MUSINGS OF MANNARKOIL PROFESSOR:

Now and then Here and there

By
G. Srinivasan

Acknowledgement

This book is a collection of autobiographical anecdotes and memories of me- a village boy from Mannarkoil, in India currently leading a retired life in Mississauga Canada. In this collection I have narrated the experiences in a humorous way covering a variety of settings. Barring a few instances I have used the real names of people-this includes my family, friends, teachers and neighbours--and my thanks are due to them for providing me with rich experience

My thanks are due to my dorm mates of yesteryears who had read some part of the work and encouraged me. My friend Professor Venkat Rao encouraged me to bring the work to wider forums. Thanks to his encouragement I got two of the sections (Chapters 9 and 11) published in the blog platform 'Twists & Twain'.

My special thanks to are due to my former professor, Dr. Shreekant Sambrani. Two years ago, he happened to read my writings on how my name gets twisted. He appreciated my style and shared his own interesting experiences with respect to his name. From then on, I have had several fruitful exchanges with him and he planted in me the idea of coming up with a collection of connected essays. My profound thanks are due to my good friend Meena Raghunathan who meticulously read the manuscript in a short time and provided several editorial and culture-sensitive comments. Those comments helped a lot in improving the presentation.

The project team at Native Book Publishing did an excellent job in bringing this book in a timely and professional manner. The editorial team, cover designers and illustrators did a wonderful job in understanding the cultural nuances presented in the book. My special thanks to Emily Wilson who made the workflow smooth and seamless.

Being the last of nine kids in my family, I had rich experiences with my parents, brothers and sisters. Having lost my father at the age of ten, it was my brother Krishnan, a lawyer, who took care of the family and gave me good education. The one next to him, Rajamannar motivated me to keep pursuing higher studies. His sharing of his experiences in U.K., Canada and Costa Rica was very inspirational. Raman the engineer brother is a humorous writer himself. He is a great motivator for my creative writing. My immediate elder brother Rengan was just one year senior to me in school. I had several wonderful years of walking with him to go to school. A good number of childhood experiences I have narrated are shared experiences. To all of them I owe a lot.

My special thanks are to Kalyani, my wife and life partner for the last forty years. She had shared with me a lot of interesting childhood experiences she had with her sisters, parents and cousins. She is a great storyteller herself. Her narration of the imaginary characters created by her cousin Ramu and herself would make the kids around go into splits.

She is my first sounding board and her help in sharpening my ideas is beyond words. She enjoys my humor and is equally candid in telling me what does and does not work. When I was ambivalent about the project, she was the one who provided me all the motivation and emotional support to complete this work.

My daughter Ragini was one of my main sources of learning. When she was growing up, I used to compare in my mind her childhood days and mine, and that is getting reflected in my writings. I have read to and read with her a number of stories written by the master story teller of India, R.K.Narayanan. Inspiration from those stories made me focus on honing the skill to paint a verbal picture. Ragini also took time to read and comment on the pieces.

It is to Kalyani, Ragini the two loves of my life and the MAGP (Mannarkoil A GopalaIyengar and Ponnuammal) clan this work is dedicated.

Prologue:
Road Map

Each chapter in this book is self-contained and can be read and enjoyed independently of others. At the same time, several of the places and persons may appear in multiple chapters. In this prologue, I provide a road map of my journey from Mannarkoil to Mississauga. In the process, I take you to some key places that I lived in, introduce you to some key persons, and share with you some key moments of my life.

My village, like many South Indian villages, was defined by its temple. The legend goes that a Chera king who renounced the kingdom and took to composing and singing the praise of Lord Vishnu founded the temple at Mannarkovil. Temples in South India typically face the east. The street in front of the temple is called the Sannathi Street, and the streets on the south, west and north sides of the temple wall are called the Maada Street. The next outer streets are typically the' Ratha Veethi' or Car Streets, where the temple rath (chariot) would be taken around with the deity during the rath festival. The Sannathi street may intersect the east car street and go beyond.

The house where I was born was in the Sannathi street. My forefathers might have been some of the early occupants of the street. The first ten or so houses in the street belonged to my father's first or second cousins and in each household, there was someone named Gopalan, a shortened form of the name of the deity of our village, Rajagopalan. I was the last of the nine kids (seven boys and two girls surviving at that time) of Gopala Iyengar and Ponnu Ammal. My father was an independent contractor undertaking to build the public works department (PWD)--projects such as building roads and bridges in the neighbourhood. As the neighbouring town, Amabsamudram was a Taluka (a subdivision of a district for administrative purposes) headquarters with a PWD office, government treasury and banks, he bought a house in Ambasamudram and moved there.

I started my primary education in Ambasamudram. Let me qualify that. I refused to go to school until I was eight years old. The reason was not that I did not like going to school. Rather I liked a particular teacher who was living opposite our house and insisted I would go only to her class and she was teaching grade three. The teacher's name was Avoodaiamma, but we knew her by a different name. Tall, well built with a smiling face and a big bindhi, she was charming. It was my routine in the morning to watch her leave for school with her hair tied into a bun. Her husband was the headmaster of the school, and they were living just opposite to our house. She used to come to our house to get something from my mother or simply for a chit-chat. We used to go to her house, and she would give us some snacks. She was the mother of four girls and a firm believer in girl's education and independence. Her youngest one was in high school at that time, and her name was Gnaanam. So we called the teacher Gnaanaththamma meaning 'mother of Gnaanam'. As I was adamant, I had to wait till I was eight to join grade three taught by her. Though I was not going to school I was learning the alphabet, multiplication tables etc., from my parents and sisters. Hence, I was more than ready for grade three. Gnaanaththammma, assessing my calibre, wanted me to work towards becoming a district collector in the Indian Administrative Service. That was a quantum jump in the aspiration level at that time.

Though we were living in Ambasamudram, which was three miles away from my village, we used to visit the village regularly. My delayed school entrance gave a lot of time for me to do so. One of my elder brothers was living in the family home and managing the family farmlands. Frequently one of father's workers would go to the village in a bicycle and I would hitch a ride. I also spent a longer time in the village during summer holidays enjoying the harvest season and temple festivals.

When I started my grade six, we had moved out of Aambasamudram to Palayamkottai, near the district headquarters, Tirunelveli. My brother (number three) was starting his legal practice there and my dad had reduced his work and moved with him to Palayamkottai. But within two years my father passed away, and we were with our lawyer brother. The 'we' consisted of two of my brothers (number five and six), the younger one of my two sisters waiting to get married, my mother and myself. Within two years my elder sister lost her husband and she, along with her four boys, ranging from four months old to ten years old moved in with us. My brother- in-law had no other siblings, and his widowed mother was living with him. On his demise, she also moved in with us. In a short while, the other sister got married and left us, even as my brother got married, and my sister-in-law joined us. Thus, during my schooldays, our household consisted of eleven members split into three widows (my mother, sister and her mother-in-law), six boys (my immediate elder brother, four nephews and myself), and a couple (my brother and his wife).

A few years later, when I was in my second year of B.Com., my lawyer-brother moved to Chennai to practice law at the High Court of Tamil Nadu. My immediate elder brother was in his final year of his science degree. Two other brothers were already in Chennai, one (number four) was pursuing a Ph.D at I.I.T, and another (number five) was working in an engineering firm. My immediate elder brother on completing his degree, moved to Chennai looking for a job and I followed him a year later.

In Chennai I was with my brother and joined a Chartered Accountant (C.A) firm, M/s S.Viswanathan as an articled clerk. As a first-class degree holder, I was in an accelerated program requiring only three instead of four years of work under the supervision of an authorized CA, before I could become one. In parallel, I had to pass the intermediate and final examination of the Institute of Chartered Accountants. The eligibility to sit for the examination required a certain minimum period of work experience in the C.A firm. After working for an year, I had appeared for the C.A. (Intermediate) exam.

Just a few days after the exam, I got a mail from the Union Bank Of India. This was in response to my application, which I had sent more than a year earlier prior to my joining the C.A. firm. They had called me to appear for an interview at Bombay (Mumbai). The letter indicated that the bank would reimburse second-class railway fare and pay a small allowance. Though I was not looking for a job, as I had joined the C.A program, I was tempted by the prospect of seeing Bombay at someone else's expense and that too travelling in second class. That was a luxury in those days. The second-class compartments provided a cushioned sleeping berth and the coaches would be a little cleaner than the third class.

I took a week off for my trip. I had earlier written to my classmate Sundaresan who was doing C.A in Bombay about my plan. He was living with his brother, and the family was kind enough to accommodate me. I had a good time with him for a couple of days. As I was fresh from my

C.A.(Inter) exam preparations, I did very well in the interview. Besides, as I was not looking for the job, I was not nervous. I came back and joined the audit team to visit Seshasayee Paper Mills at Erode. I totally forgot about my interview with Union Bank. Given the time lag between my application and interview, I was not expecting any intimation from them for at least a year

At Seshasayee mills, I met an interesting officer in the Cost Accounting section, and my seniors have told me he was an excellent palm reader. In one of the lunch breaks my friends took me to him. After a few minutes of reading my palm, he told us that I would be having a break in my studies. My friends were aghast. Thinking that he implied I might not pass the Inter exam and leave, they told him I was one of the brightest in the firm and had obtained the article clerk position reserved for first-class graduates. The chip of the palmist went down drastically in the minds of my seniors.

A few days after returning to Chennai from Erode, in early December of 1972, I received a mail from Union Bank asking me to visit their regional office. The time specified for the visit was after the regular office hours. I could not make much sense of it. If the meeting were to be in a regular branch, I could understand that branch would be busy with customers during regular hours. But the office of a Personnel Officer (Human Resource these days) was not expected to be crowded. In any event, the office was in Kurlagam buildings which was next door to my C.A office in Esplanade. I visited the office and was greeted by an assistant to the Personnel Officer. She indicated that as a follow-up to my interview, I needed to undergo a medical examination. She would not confirm whether I was selected for the job, nor would she tell me how long it would take for a decision. She handed over a sealed envelope addressed to a doctor and told me I should visit him within three days for a medical examination. She also indicated that the matter was confidential. Suddenly, I was in a thick soup, wondering what I should be doing if I was selected for the job. But I quickly set those thoughts aside, considering they might take another year to decide.

Within a few days I received another mail to meet the Personnel Officer (P.O) on the 26th of December evening. Mr. Uma Maheswaran, the P.O., greeted me and took me to his office. After closing the door, he showed me the seat. Sitting face to face, he congratulated me, informing me that I was selected as a probationary officer. Passing the papers to my side, he indicated that the offer was valid, provided I could join the bank at the Tirunelveli branch (five miles away from Palayamkottai, where I was living before coming to Chennai) on or before the 29th, and I needed to sign the papers then and there. Tirunelveli was about 400 miles south of Chennai, and it would take fourteen hours to reach there by bus or train. That implied If I were to take the job, I had to leave Chennai the very next evening. I felt cornered.

I was working for my C.A., but that required another two years at the C.A firm The Probationary Officer with Union Bank of India was a high-paying job at that time (started with a salary of Rs. 350 per month and an allowance for inflation of Rs.150). Considering the fact that my brother had been shouldering family responsibilities for a long time, accepting the job was tempting. When I had discussed the possibility of getting the job with the family after the medical exam, all my brothers assured me that they would support my continuing C.A., but left the decision to me. My immediate elder brother had got a job in a similar bank but at a much junior level and indicated it would take seven years for him to reach the officer level. All these factors and also the fact that the posting would be in Tirunelveli was very tempting, as I could join the house of three mothers who had lost their husbands, as a bread winner. But not having time to think was very annoying, even though I had had an inkling that I would get the job.

At the spur of the moment, I thought I could play 'the auspicious time' card. Even though I had no particular faith, I knew elders in our family used to consult astrologers and almanac for all major decisions to make sure things started at an auspicious time. Sometimes, there would even be a pooja or prayer session prior to those events. I told Mr. Uma Maheswaran I needed a few days before accepting the job as I needed to check for an auspicious time for accepting it. He just lifted his head up from the papers he was showing me and told in a gentle, elderly voice.

"Young man, in a country where thousands are waiting for years even to get an acknowledgment for their application, the time you get a good job is an auspicious time, and you need no astrologer to tell you that."

That was a moment that is still vivid in my memory. I thanked him and signed the paper He indicated that the joining date was firm and asked me to make necessary arrangements quickly and keep everything low-key. I took the appointment order in hand, and as I was walking, I saw another young man in the waiting room. Mentally, I thought he might be my backup. As I got out of the building, I was shaking. I went and got a bottle of Neera (non-alcoholic toddy) from the shop in the ground floor. Sipping the drink, I chalked out a plan of action.

The long-distance bus stand was just opposite to the building. I walked over there and bought a bus ticket for the next night. I went home and informed my brothers of my decision to join the bank, and that I needed to leave the next day. Luckily, as I was going back to my previous home, where a lot of my things were still there, my packing was minimal. The next morning I went to the C.A firm and told them I was leaving. Mr. Chandru, my boss, was disappointed but understood my decision. I filed the papers for them to relieve me and left. I could not even see my friends to say bye, and till date, I have not met any of my fellow article clerks. At the back of my mind I was thinking of the Erode palmist. His prediction had come true in the sense that the break was not due to my failing in the exam but due to voluntarily leaving.

That night I left for Tirunelveli with my bedding and plate, among other things. Yes, from my childhood, I had my own stainless steel plate (no silver platter though!) with my name on it. I had carried it with me while moving to Chennai and I was taking that back. I landed in my house around 7.30 a.m., and my mother was shocked. Seeing me arrive there without notice and with my bedding and plate, my mother thought I must have had a fight with my brother and left his house in anger. I just told her I was in a hurry and asked her to be calm. I had a quick wash and then left. I knew the Union Bank was very close to the Tirunelveli Bus station. A city bus took me within five minutes and I was there at the bank by 9 a.m. on the 28th. The bank used to open for business at 10 a.m., but the manager, Mr. Ramarao, was there. I knocked at his door, and he quickly took me in. It appeared he was expecting me. I gave him the papers and soon, the formalities of joining the bank were done. As the staff started coming in, the manager introduced me to them as the new officer joining the branch. He requested their help as I would need training at all the counters. The staff members were perplexed. As the bank year was ending in a couple of days, they even questioned the wisdom of joining at the year-end when all of them would be very busy and would have no time to attend to a trainee.

The next morning, the employee's union representative of the branch received a telegram from the union headquarters asking him to prevent the new officer from joining the bank. He patted my shoulder and told me that I had escaped. Then he explained that the bank was exercising its right to recruit officers directly thus denying promotion opportunities to the staff. Though the right was negotiated a few years earlier, it was not implemented thus far, and the agreement was ending at the end of the year. It was then that I understood why the whole process had been so secretive. Later, I gathered that there were about a dozen or so people recruited that year who joined the bank a day before the last working day of the year due to this reason. After about three weeks of joining, I got my C.A. (inter) result. I had cleared the exam. I had obtained twenty-third rank nationally. Though my seniors at the firm were correct in assessing my calibre, the palmist at the paper mill might have had his last laugh. I had returned to the house of three mothers who had lost their husbands, but this time as breadwinner.

My brother Rajamannar was not happy that I left my professional education. However, he advised me to enhance my expertise in my job. To that end he enrolled me in the Institute of Bankers London as a student member. The fee in British Pound was quite hefty. I took his advice seriously and cleared the intermediate exam which even got me an increment in my salary. While working in the bank, I also completed the Master's Program of Sri Venkateswara University, which did not have the residency requirement.

In the Bank, my work in the audit cell required travel to various cities and doing surprise audits. Our travel schedule was known only to very few in the audit cell and was dynamic in the sense while working in a branch there might be a directive to do a surprise audit the next day in another branch hundreds of miles away.

It was almost three years since I had joined the bank when I came across an advertisement for the Fellow Program (that was how the IIM Doctoral title was called then) of the Indian Institute of Management (IIMA).Till then I had not heard of IIMA. The scholarship amount offered was sufficient to cover the tuition, boarding and lodging and leave some for expenses. And, of course, they were paying second-class fare for the interview. As one of my nephews had finished his degree and was ready for a job, and other nephews were grown up and doing well at school, I felt that my leaving the job would not create too much of a hole in the family finances. Hence, I thought I could think of a doctoral program as I had completed my Masters. There was an admission test prior to the interview, and I decided to appear for the same. Only when I was talking to some of the students at the examination hall did I realize that IIMA was the top institute of management in India and had a collaboration of Harvard, and that getting admission would not be that easy. If only I had known that, I would have perhaps done some special preparation for the test. But on the positive side, I was under no pressure as I already had a good job.

I was in the audit department of the bank, and my boss was one Mr. Ramankutty. I asked him whether he knew about IIMA. He knew so much that he advised me that I would not regret it if I left the bank to pursue the program at IIMA.

I had cleared the admission test of IIMA and got a call for a personal interview, When I received the notice, I was visiting a branch that was close to Kanyakumari, the southernmost part of the state. Train travel to Ahmedabad would take three nights and two days and would be hectic. Mr. Ramankutty was very accommodating in rescheduling my work. I flew into Bombay from Chennai so that I could attend the interview in time. Though the free second-class railway travel was an attraction at the time of my application, I ended up spending a lot more But every paise (penny equivalent) was worth it, as IIMA made a significant difference in my life. I finished the four-year program and on completion, was selected to be a Faculty Member there. After a long time, the Institute made an exemption that year to their policy of not hiring their own graduates immediately on graduation. After working there for two years, I got an assignment at the University of

New Brunswick (UNB) Canada, where I was a Visiting Faculty for two years. After spending two years in Canada, I returned home, got married and rejoined IIMA. After three more years at IIMA, I got an offer from UNB for a permanent position. Accepting that, my wife and I moved to Fredericton Canada, as permanent residents. After teaching about three and a half decades at UNB, I took retirement to settle in the city of Mississauga. And that is where we are now.

There are a lot of interesting stories to narrate from my IIMA days and UNB days. But that is left to a later date. The road map provided above would help you to connect the places and people you may come across in the next thirteen chapters. Let's take off.

GS

Contents

Chapter 1 What is there in the name?

Recently I read a joke in a WhatsApp forwards on the English spelling of the word diarrhoea against the American spelling of diarrhea, commenting that the English one appears to have lost control of vowels. Apart from making a quick comment as to whether they lost control of vowels or bowels, I started thinking about my encounters with spelling and pronunciation.

When I moved to Fredericton, Canada, in the '80s, the first thing I realized was that the south Indian, especially Tamilians who had eliminated their caste from their names, suffered from a disease called 'lack of last name' syndrome. I had to explain that Srinivasan was my first name, and the G, my initial, stood for the first name of my father, Gopalan. I used to tell people they should be happy I had not included another initial M for my village, Mannarkoil. They would have gone crazy if I were to write Mannarkoil Gopala Iyengar Srinivasan. That was not just a name but an entire address. Srinivasan, son of Gopala Iyengar of Mannarkoil, is, in my mind, a complete address. This is not any narcissistic thinking--that everyone should know Mannarkoil. Rather, it is acknowledging that our world was limited to a ten-mile radius where every villager knew the ten surrounding villages! Thank God I did not mention to them that my nick name at home was Mohan.

Because I was born on the second of October, the birthdate of the Father of the Nation, Mohandas Gandhi, they called me Mohan. Perhaps they had started with Gandhi Mohan and dropped the Gandhi part after I started telling lies! If my colleagues from the social science department had heard this, they would have immediately written a research proposal on the topic of 'Naming practices of the South Indian community' and would have obtained a nice grant.

Just as they would go crazy with the long name, I would be equally annoyed if they had called me Mannarkoil, thinking that they are on a first-name basis. (Incidentally, the South Indian custom with respect to female names does not face these issues as the father's name or husband's name comes at the end and becomes the natural last name.)

Another interesting consequence of the Lack of Last Name syndrome was the emergence of 'first name twice' remedy. It was common among South Indian academics working in the U.S.A. to solve the problem in a unique way, they truncated their first name and made it the first name, and used the longer version of the first name as the last name, as in Bala Balachandran, Kas Kasturi, and the like. I started using Sri Srinivasan. I think Pizza Pizza copied from us, perhaps. When President Obama was considering nominating one Sri Srinivasan for the Supreme Court, people used to ask me whether I was related. I had to educate them that in that part of the world, Srinivasan is the first name; one might find thousands with the name who may not be related at all. Later, when I attended a conference in India, they introduced me as Sri Srinivasan, the first Sri denoting 'Mr'! That was the very time when religious gurus were fighting as to how many sris they should have in front of their name. Right then I decided not to go the Sri Srini route.

After convincing, cajoling, or commanding my colleagues to stick to only Srinivasan and, at the most, the shorter form, Srini, I found at the next-level problems with spelling and pronunciation.

My wife was a practicing family physician. As a part of her duties, she would be on call some nights, making herself available to attend to the medical emergencies of patients who had been admitted to the hospital by doctors belonging to her group. Typically, she would make an evening round and assess the need, discuss with the attending nurses the general plan for each patient and return home by 10 p.m. She would be carrying a pager, and if there was any need, she would be paged. Whenever she was paged, I would also be woken (luckily, I have the gift of getting back to sleep in spite of interruption). Most days, she could address the issues by phone as it might only involve some calibration of dosage or ordering some diagnostic test, etc.

One day, after a page from the hospital, she talked over the phone for a minute and then told me that she had to go to the hospital as she had to pronounce. I was perplexed as to what she meant. She repeated that she had to pronounce Paul Smith. I was at a loss. I was aghast and asked her why the native English speakers did not know how to pronounce Paul Smith and needed to call her in the middle of the night. She laughed and laughed and explained that in t medical lingo, 'pronouncing' meant pronouncing someone dead, and a nurse was not authorized to do the same. Furthermore, unless pronounced, they could not proceed with funeral arrangements, and hence, she needed to go in the middle of the night to pronounce. After that day, whenever someone asked me as to how they should pronounce my name, I simply said, "Please don't. I am alive."

Spelling my name is another whole story. The English language does not have a single word that starts with 'Sr'. Hence people automatically assumed I had made a mistake when I printed my name in forms. My provincial health card carried three different spellings--one each for my daughter, wife, and me. The narrow boxes where we printed each letter might have given credence to their belief that I had made some mistake. One box where the right side curve of the letter' r' touched the top of the box made them believe that it was a 'p', and they were happy to put it that way. And in another, the stem line of 'r' was split a little bit, which made them assume that the letter was a 'v', and in third one, they might have thought there must be a mistake and changed the 'r' to 'c'. So the card had Spinivasan, Svinivasan and Scinivasan. Take your pick, Srini!

At that point, I tried to understand how that could happen, and that was when I realized that there was no word in English beginning with 'Sr'. Probably in the typist examinations, the key for 'R' must have been programmed not to move forward after the strike of an 'S' unless there was another keystroke in between. Better still, maybe the letter 'R' moves backward if struck after 'S' and hits the forehead of the typist, marking an impression of 'R' on it, and examiners can reject the candidate just by looking at the forehead.

No wonder, the first thing the English did on coming to Sri Lanka was to change the name to Ceylon. Maybe thinking that Sri Lanka is an Epsilon addition to their bigger colony India, they might have named it Ceylon, little realizing that Sri Lanka was as big as Scotland. Whatever the reason, the fact remained that in their grammar, 'r' does not follow an 's' in a word without an intervener.

Furthermore, a number of forms would arbitrarily cut my name off as it exceeded the space limit. A language pathologist diagnosed that I was suffering from hypervowel syndrome. (It was rumored that my colleagues from Poland were diagnosed with hypovowel syndrome)

It is not only in official forms that I saw my name tarnished or varnished. In the examination booklet, students had to write the course number and instructor's name. My name would be on the question paper for them to see. In spite of that, I would find all kinds of spellings for my name.

I can understand that some might have thought I was hopping in the class from isle to isle in a slightly stooped manner and that it would be nice to add some spine and make me Spinivasan.

Others could have been wondering when my course would be over and they could bury me and build a shrine, and hence made me a Shrinivasan. An occasional student from India would make it Shreeni. In all, I had multiple Avatars.

Not all my experiences were that bad. . I was attending an academic conference in Xian, China, organized by CIDA

Canada. There were hundreds of participants. Anyone I met, I would tell them my name and quickly, before they could ask any further questions, lift my name tag up so that they could read it. I was in the elevator with another American gentleman and I said hello and introduced myself as Srini. He responded by saying 'Oh, Srinivasan' and I was surprised and told him I was. He responded by saying that he worked in Carnegie and that he could not be there without knowing the name Srinivasan. The elevator opened then, and he was getting off on that floor before I could hear him say his name. However, I glanced at his tag which said 'Simon', and it was in a different colour. That night, I figured out he was the keynote speaker Herbert Simon, the Nobel laureate!

From time to time, I would have a student or two who would pronounce my name correctly. Upon inquiry as to how they had managed to do so, they would reveal that my wife was their doctor. A few years ago--that was after thirty-six years at UNB-- on the first day of the course, a student approached me after the class, addressing me correctly. I expressed my surprise that he could say my name well on day one itself. That is when he told me that looking at his course registration, his mother had told him how my name had to be pronounced. Upon further questioning he told me that his mother had taken the same course from me three decades earlier. That was when it struck me that I would be having 'grand-students' in my class.

That was my Eureka moment. The very same day, I went to the Dean's office and informed him of my decision to retire. He tried to convince me otherwise. I told him it would be very difficult for me to prepare for the course. He chided me, saying, "Srini, what preparations do you need? You have teaching this course for decades. You can deliver the course even in your sleep."

And I replied that this was exactly the problem. I had no worries about preparing for the course content. But I was getting grand-students, and I needed to prepare a whole new set of jokes and anecdotes, as the current students must have heard the same from their parents.

I cannot start the class with, "Hello, I am Srinvasan," with a tongue-twisting name in a tiny frame, as that would not be novel anymore.

Nor would they laugh when I cracked a joke about my handwriting, saying hieroglyphics was being taught at no extra cost.

And the days I lost my voice, I could not go on with my standard limerick.

My throat is sore

and my voice cannot soar.

But that does not mean

You can sleep and snore.

And the list went on.

Now, I am a retired professor looking for a new market for the old stuff!

And I found you.

PS The problem of pronunciation is not always a one-way street in the sense that only I am at the receiving end. My language, Tamil, uses the same first letter for Gandhi, Kaalidasa, or Cauvery, (the sounds 'g', 'k' and 'c' are denoted by the same problem) so you can see my problem!

Chapter 2 A Journey From Slate Pencil to Real Pencil

It all started when I was four years old or so on an auspicious Vijaya Dasami day (the day to start formal education). We were gathered in front of our 'Perumal sannathi' (pooja room), where on a wooden plank decorated with 'kolam' (rangoli without colour), a cup of paddy was spread. Appa held my index finger and wrote the word

"Hari Om" on the paddy, signifying an auspicious beginning. It is the same index finger I used to write on the paddy that I use even today to punch the letters in my keyboard or the touch computer screen. Between these index finger eras, there are a handful of writing instruments and mediums that I have used. This is an attempt to capture some of those memories.

The first major medium for writing I used was the metallic 'slate'--a thin black tin plate in a wooden frame. As the real slate made of the rock material would be a little heavier and easily breakable, only the tin slate was given to beginners. The stuff to write with, the slate- pencil, or stylus in modern lingo, is called 'kuchchi' (குச்சி) in our part of the deep southern districts. In Madras, they call it Palappam (பலப்பம்). On a tin slate, nothing would work well. One needed chalk or a chalk-like thick kuchhi. The black coating on the tin would start wearing off quickly. My demand for a new real slate would be brushed away with some sarcastic comments like, "For the amount of writing you do, this is more than enough," or, "You cannot carry the weight." However, there would be a promise of a new slate for the next grade.

Moving to use a real slate was a big promotion. Apart from the traditional slate pencil (made up of slate rock powder), we also used a sharp bone/thorn-like material from sea urchins. (As a Brahmin, I thought it was from a sea plant).

We used to call it "kadal kuchchi' (slate pencil from the sea). It used to be greenish in colour with a pointed end and a head like a pin. It was very good for sharp and bright writing. With the regular slate pencil, letters would be a bit thicker. The worst thing with the slate pencil was some sharp particles in it would make an unbearable nail-scratching noise. That unpleasant memory was well etched in my mind. So much so, in one of my graduate classes, when the chalk used by my professor created the same noise, I was jolted and requested him to stop the class for a minute.

During the first few weeks, cleaning the slate with water was a fun activity. I felt important. Doing it gave me a sense of ownership, pride, and responsibility. We also used some green 'kovai' (ivy gourd plant) leaves to wipe the slate clean and then gave it a wash. Those green leaves were the Ayurvedic tonic for the slate. Just like cast iron skillets were tempered with oil, our slates were tempered with the extract of a special leaf. Slate being porous, perhaps the extract helped to keep the surface smooth.

Every year, within about three months of the school year, a crack would appear on the slate. The first time when that happened, one felt sad and worried about parental reactions. Quietly, I would approach Mom when my dad was not around, show the slate, and complain that I did not know how it happened. (Of course, the fact I had thrown the school bag carelessly would not be told). She would glance at it like a doctor would at a patient and declare that I could manage with that slate till the next year. She was experienced enough to assess the situation quickly. After all, she had raised eight other kids before me, who had all perhaps given her the same excuse and got from her the same verdict and sentence.

Just when I felt comforted, one of the big brothers would scare me with the declaration," Oh, the corner piece will come off in a week, and there will be a big hole."

Then came the pencil age. The pencil-Paper age was and is altogether a different experience.

The pencil-notebook stage was a big deal in the progression. In addition to a notebook and a pencil, one needed to have a few other accessories--the eraser and the sharpener. Pencils came in different grades. Most of my childhood, I got to use only the run-of-the-mill, no name brand cylindrical yellow wood coloured pencil--that too, not a full-length one. Dad used to get them in bulk. Some of the pencils would be cut in half so that the younger ones could handle them easily.

Dad would show his prowess by sharpening the pencil with a knife. I used to watch in admiration with a dropped jaw. There was a strict protocol. I was not allowed to stand in front. He did not want me to have the pencil shavings for breakfast. He would sharpen it to an optimum level where it was neither so sharp that it would break, nor so flat that the pencil would make double lines.

As I grew older, I was given a sharpener so that I could do my own sharpening. The sharpener was not of top-notch quality. Often it would break the tip of the pencil just around the time when you thought you were done. Actually, and perhaps appropriately, we used to call the device a cutter. It was much later I learnt that it was called a sharpener!

The cutter I had was one of the cheap plastic ones bought for half an anna (three paise). To give an idea, the cool metallic one cost four and a half annas, and that was the price of one pound of sugar in our ration shop! I still remember the green transparent plastic frame of my sharpener. A round mouth wide enough to get the pencil in, a narrowing body with a slit in the middle, and a covered tail tip completed the broad picture of it. Under the slit on one side, was a tiny silver-coloured saw-toothed blade. The mechanism was simple. After inserting the pencil at the mouth part of the cutter, one needed to push it through the narrowing tunneled middle, where the blade would do the job of removing the obstacle. As we pushed the pencil, wood shavings would jet out of the slit in a neat curly form. Those shavings were one of the feedstocks for the peacock feather tucked in a book. It was the prevalent myth which we all firmly believed that a peacock feather would multiply if we fed them such sundry things as pencil shavings.

Once the lead part of the pencil (I have no idea why the carbon middle was called lead and the pencil a lead pencil) got exposed, the nice pastel colour shavings would be marred by graphite dust. But the pencil would come out with a nice shape, an inverted cone on top of a cylinder. After blowing the dust off the sharpener and keeping it safe, one was ready to put the pencil to use.

During the writing process, a part of the pencil resting on the side of the thumb and the distal joint of the index finger would be flexed to make almost forty-five degrees to get a good grip. Such a grip was recommended for good handwriting. Holding it tight, one would start writing. Just about when you felt elated, the tip of the pencil would break. The attempt to somehow fit the broken tip back into the pencil would only add to the frustration. Trying with one's nail to peel off a little bit of wood to expose some more of the lead would offer only temporary relief. Occasionally, the rough edges would poke the nail bed, extracting a small drop of blood and resulting in a reflexive suction treatment.

It was probably a month or so after the first experience. I was in a hurry to get the pencil sharpened. I pushed the pencil into the sharpener, held it tight, and started rotating the pencil fast. In a few seconds, I heard a creaking noise and saw the mouth part of the plastic frame developing a crack. That was the end of Sharpener Grundy. (I was reminded of Solomon Grundy born on Monday...).

I had watched my elder brothers sharpen their pencils with a razor blade. I thought it was time for me to graduate. One day, I quietly went to the cupboard where Dad used to keep his shaving materials. There was a pile of yellow wrapper. Inside, there was another wax paper wrap guarding the Panama blade. Among the few blades that were there, I picked the one that had shown some rust on one side of the blade. It appeared he might have kept it for a few more shaves, as the other side was rust-free. I made an executive decision that my needs were more important. I assumed that he might not notice it, as there were a few more blades in the pile. Besides, I had seen him a few days earlier bringing home a few grey packs of 7' O clock blades. Those were brought from Colombo by a friend who made frequent business trips to Sri Lanka..

It was not easy at that time to sharpen neatly the pencil with a blade. Sharp, tiny pieces of wood chips substituted the nice, curly, well-bordered shavings, thus denying food to the peacock feather. Further, the accidental nicks resulted in a few drops of bloodshed, needing an emergency sucking and saliva treatment... Maybe it was these experiences that might have worked on me for a while. Arriving in Canada about three decades later, one of my very early purchases was an electric sharpener. It did not give me the curly shavings either, but was efficient and safe. Besides, I did not have the peacock feather to feed!

The story of the eraser, which we simply called a rubber, was equally fascinating. They came in different shapes. White, thin, rectangular, or square slabs and thicker, roundish ones were commonly available. At home, there was a bigger trapezium shaped eraser with half the surface white in colour and the other half pink. The pink side was supposed to be useful for erasing pen marks. In school, some kids had colourful scented erasers. They had some relatives in Colombo from where they used to get those fancy ones. Those erasers were translucent, looking more like candy. After a few days of use, the edges of our white erasers would be black in colour and would not work well. The treatment for that was very simple. We used to rub those edges on a white-washed wall.

We had a front corridor wall that was taking all such abuses. At the top of the wall, the NMEP (National Malaria Eradication Program) people would have drawn a table to mark the dates of their visits and spraying of DDT. At another corner, our dahi vendor would have placed a few dots indicating our purchases. Each dot represented a certain quantity of dahi supplied. She would settle the account at the month's end. Somewhere in between, we would locate some white spots and give a couple of quick rubs to our eraser, and it would get energized.

From the no-brand half pencil, I moved to Nataraj pencils. The pencils with their name and place of manufacture gave printed shavings. It would be fun to reassemble those words from the shavings. In the class, there were kids that had green-coloured hexagonal pencils made in Germany. Of course, a lot of us were green with envy. I had a liking for pencils. (Still do.) I used to admire with awe when my brother used to get numbered pencils for his engineering drawing (HB2, HB1, etc).

When I moved to Canada, I was thrilled to see the amount of pencil usage. More than 80% of my students used pencils for their notes, assignments, and exams. As a standard, most of the pencils came with the eraser attached at the end. I used to admire the aspirational goal embedded in those pencils. If the tiny eraser were to last for the entire life of the pencil one should be writing almost flawlessly. The fact that Canada is primarily a country of softwood lumber and rubber is not its native plant may explain the pencil length and the tiny eraser end. In addition, pencils are dead cheap in Canada -literally a dime a dozen. Almost like an addict I used to buy in dozens even though I had a free supply of pencils in my office.

I worked with a philosophy that there should not be a hardware bottleneck. Hence, I had several pencils sharpened and ready, whether I had something to write about or not. I never had to count my pencil usage thanks to the generous supply from the school. However, I had worked in a situation where I had to account for every pencil.

That was fifty years ago when I was an articled clerk in the C.A. firm M/s S. Viswanathan. The firm used brown colour pencils for audit marks and they were kept under lock and key. When we went out for an audit, we would sign and, take pencils and bring back the stubs. That was an internal control mechanism. A pencil left at the client site would facilitate them to make marks as if we had checked those entries. And, of course, we were prohibited from using any eraser. If we had made a mistake, we simply were asked to put a dot above the audit line and later connect the dot to the line when rectified. The brown pencil was the cultural icon of the firm, so much so the telegraphic address of the firm was simply a browntick. Yes, there was something called telegraphic address in those days!

Though I had a fascination for mechanical pencils, I never found them user-friendly. It was very difficult to get the desired length of the lead and it used to break often. The only attraction I found was they came with a clip and were easy to carry in a shirt pocket.

As I have said, I love pencils. They are great for doodling while you sit in a boring committee meeting. When stuck on ideas (or lack thereof), I used to decorate the borders of the pages of the writing pad with several untitled doodles. Upon retirement, along with my books I had brought home several writing pads with half-baked ideas and untitled doodles. I was telling my wife that mathematician Fermat scribbled his conjecture in the margin of a sheet, and it took centuries for people to prove it, and similarly, it will take a while for people to interpret my 'untitled' doodles Who knows, if 'doodlism' becomes the next hot genre of art, I might have some master pieces!.

About my experience with pens- I should pen something in one of these days. Let me pencil it in my calendar.

Chapter 3 The Haircut

As I was caressing my long tresses of Corona lockout hair, I dozed off. My dream took me far away to my childhood haircut experience.

When I was a young boy, barber Paramasivan used to come home for Appa's haircut. He would open his shop inside our verandah. On his getting ready, he would unload articles from his bag one by one slowly, as a magician would do: an aluminum bowl, a brush with a white handle with the name Palmolive (popular those days), a knife, and a thick leather-like thing to sharpen the knife as it made clapping noise. It was a show by itself.

Appa hardly had that much hair on his head, which warranted a visit by Paramasivan. All he had was a mere crescent on the vast, shiny expanse of his occiput. Primarily barber's visit was for a light trimming at the back and for an underarm shave. That would not take much time, and that was the problem. To leverage his visit, some vaandus (young kids in Tamil) would be drafted to have a haircut.

There, sitting by the side, I would be admiring the skill with which Paramsivam extracted a huge lather from the dry soap disc. Getting luxurious lather by a high-speed spin of the brush would remind me of the scene where Lord

Vishnu churned for the Amrita, the nectar. When Dad lifted his arm for under shave, I would be embarrassed and giggle silently, turning the other way to hide it. All that fun would come to a screeching halt when my mother would declare, "Get ready, take off your shirt. You are next."

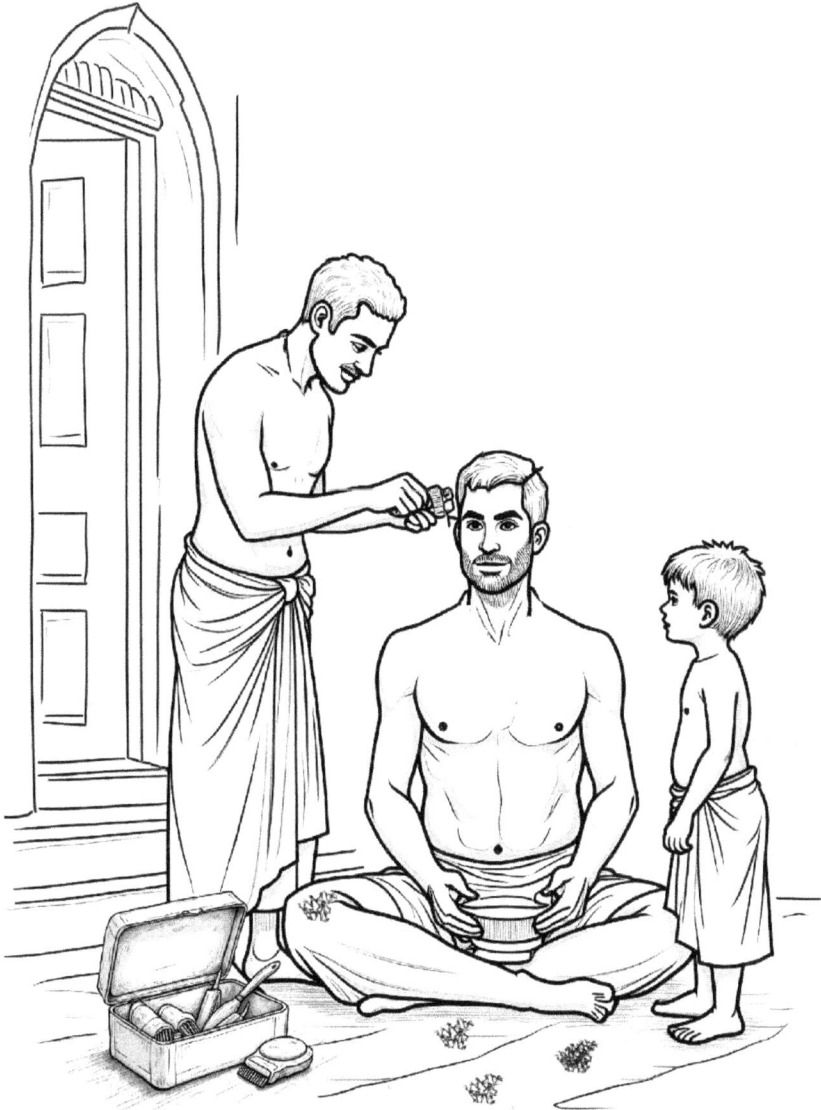

I would run in and remind my mom,"Last time you told me I can go to the salon next time to which she would calmly say 'next time.'" That reminded me of an undated perpetual notice that I used to see in our grocery shop that read, "Cash today, credit tomorrow."

Having failed in accusing, I would go to my next line of defence and plead for mercy. To my pleas of, "He makes cuts that hurt, please let me go to the salon," Mom would say, "Don't worry, I will put in a word with Paramsivam."

With that she would give a shout to him to do it gently.

Like a lamb walking to its sacrificial altar, I would slowly come out. He would clear the wooden plank and signal me to sit. Then he would pick out the "tickticki" machine (clipper) out of his bag. The old machine would look like a sea crab. His moving the handles to check whether it was working would make the tickticki noise and, hence, the name. He would adjust the ear like a screw to get the level correct. The fine teeth of the blades moving against each other would look like a thousand-toothed monster chewing its food. Inside with shiny white metal and outside in black iron colour, it would particularly be menacing.

He would dip three of his fingers in the bowl and using the wet hand, would comb through my hair. My reaction to the water drops tickling my cheeks would get a stern warning from him, "Keep your head still while I am using the machine." Thereby implying he had disowned any responsibility for the cuts that I might get.

If you were to do it gently, why would I shake my head was my silent answer. Before I realized it, he would start at a vulnerable place, exactly where I had scratched my head a little deep the previous day. As I would try to react to the sharp pain, he would hold my head with his left hand so tight that the counter-irritant technique would take my attention away from itching to a newer sensation of PAIN!

In a matter of seconds, he would do a whiff with his right hand, and a lump of wet hair would fall to my side, with a few hairs falling on my eyelashes on their way down. That would make me close my eyes. Soon, the machine sound would stop. I would have the guts to open my eyes only to see him sharpen the knife again on the leather-like thing. The scene of the knife-sharpening guy that I had witnessed a couple of days before would come to my mind. Pedalling vigorously, he would turn the wheel coated with abrasive and skillfully place the knife on the fast-moving wheel in a counter motion, creating sparks of fire. Now, the image of Paramasivan with a knife in his hand only created fear!

In the same fashion, Paramasivan would declare, "I have to clear something around your ears." With that uncontested declaration, he would start sharpening the knife and bring it close to the ear.

Being closer to the ear, the sound of the knife moving would be amplified. It was the sheer numbness out of fear that kept me still and saved me a few skin cuts.

Soon he would give a shout to my mom to come and inspect. She would step into the verandah (even without properly looking at me and much to my anguish), and she would say, "It appears nothing has been taken at all. You can cut more."

This was akin to my mother's barter trade in the morning for spinach and rice with the vegetable vendor. She would bring the rice in a big pan and split it into two heaps. The spinach vendor would take the rice and place the spinach on the pan to spread out wide. My mom, with a swift move, would get all the spinach in one hand and tell her, "Look, I gave you two handfuls of rice, and you have not given even one handful. Give more."

Of course, after that, there would be a bargain for free curry leaves, too.

It appeared Paramsivan was anticipating the comment. He would readily pick up his scissors and would do some more trimming here and there.

Then, proudly he would pick out a round mirror from his bag and show me. Seeing his knife still open, I would say 'nice,' just to deter him from doing more snipping. When he had shown me the back of my head, I would notice a small stem- an arrow pointing to my spinal cord. It reminded the bottom part of the "Thenkalai Naamam" (a Y-shaped religious mark worn on the forehead by a subset of Iyengars). I never understood that style.

Later on, when I started going to the salon for my haircut, things were not easy either. In the bazaar, there were two salons. One was operated by a trade union activist known to my brother. He would be at the doorstep of his shop, greeting us every day when we went past him. His shop had a half gate like some offices, a wooden chair. He would put a plank on its arms to increase the height. The shop next door, on the other hand, had nice glass walls, swivel chairs whose height could be adjusted without planks, glossy gossip magazines to read, and a nice spray for water.

Our sense of guilt did not allow us to skip the almost empty salon owned by the union-friendly welcoming barber to the posh but crowded next door.

Later, when I graduated using a hairdresser instead of a barber, the hairdresser asked me whether he should make it a square at the back. Without knowing anything, I answered in the affirmative. Finally, when he showed me the mirror, I was surprised and thrilled to see that the arrow pointing to my spinal cord was gone. The back was like the Tamil letter Ц. I never knew we could make a fashion statement like the ladies who talk about Ц necked blouses. That was a eureka moment. Shouting "Aha!" I got out of my nap, bringing me back to the present Corona gloom.

Hearing me shout and seeing me with my hand on my head, my wife got worried- "Look what this lockout has done to you. You are right in the looney bin," she lamented. I told her not to worry, as I knew the medicine for that illness. I immediately reached out for my computer, and out came this blurb.

Recently, in one of my post-COVID haircuts, my hairdresser started with the regular question as to where I was originally from. When I replied India she wanted to know whether south or north. After answering that I was from south India, she responded to my question that she was from Croatia and wanted to travel to India. Further, she asked whether I speak Kannada, Tamil, or Telugu. I was impressed with her knowledge. Most of the time, my conversations in similar situations have ended with Bollywood and the Khans. But the hair dresser was talking about the south Indian temples and her interest in seeing the bridge under the sea built by Lord Rama in Sethu that was sighted by a satellite. I was wonder-struck by the extent of social media that had helped in increasing awareness. As she was talking she also asked whether she could clear the hairs in my ears as that was part of the senior package. As I replied in the affirmative, I closed my eyes. I was comparing the fear I had as a child when

Paramasivan wanted to clean around my ears and the comfort with which I am allowing the trimmer to get into my ears! I could not control my smile. And that was when the hairdresser said that she forgot to mention the trimmer into the ears could be ticklish.

As I was getting down from my chair after my haircut was done, I could not but resist the scene of a small boy of Indian origin getting his haircut in the chair behind the one I was getting my haircut. His mother was on the side holding him, the father in front of him showing a comic playing on his phone, while the boy was getting his hair cut. I was about to tell the boy,' Kido, it was not that fun in my days.' But then, What do I know? Perhaps after a few years, he might in his blog complain that his parents did not take him to the salon where they had a small TV screen attached to the chair handle, or his dad could not have his hands steady, and the cartoon was jumping up and down!

Chapter 4 Back To School

The back-to-school season was always a fun time for me during the early years of growing up. The activities did not just start a couple of weeks prior to the school reopening. In fact, the clear demarcation was the day after the posting of the previous year's final examination results. That was when we were allowed to dispose of the previous year's notebooks, test papers, etc. It did not matter how confident we were of passing the exams. We were not allowed to dispose of the books and notebooks until the results were declared.

When my brothers were in high school, my father used to get us the famous "Tirunelveli Halva," made of wheat flour in pure ghee, to celebrate the success of my brothers. Given I was the last of seven brothers; there were at least two of my brothers attending high school when I was growing up. The school would announce the results for all the classes on the same day. My brothers were good in academics; there was never a situation of one passing and another failing. Hence the result day was always a celebration day.

Three significant places in my life, namely Mannarkoil, my birthplace. Ambasamudram, the town where I had my primary education, and Palayamkottai, where I spent my high school and college years, were all located in the

Tirunelveli district. That is not the reason I maintain even today that Tirunelveli Halva is the best sweet in the world. I do so because it is! The sweet vendor would place the halva on a piece of banana leaf and wrap it with what we used to call oil paper, something like wax paper. The part of the leaf that had contact with hot halva would be cooked instantly and turn pale, emanating a distinct flavour.

Dad would bring home the halva in bulk, cut it to size with a knife, and distribute it to us. We would be eagerly watching his moves. He would pick up a piece of slippery halva with his hand and place it on our extended palms. Instantly, we would feel the heat on our hands. My father used to chew paan with tobacco, that too a gooey one. Hence, it was quite likely that his hand would have some tobacco flavour. Thus, we would have had a unique blend of banana leaf and tobacco-flavoured halva. Maybe I should patent the flavor before Ben and Jerry's comes up with that for their ice cream.

The excitement the next day to clear the old notebooks was due to the fact we could sell the used papers to the sweet vendor who would buy them by weight. Yes, old papers had a market as they were used for packing. There was even a hierarchy. English newspapers like The Hindu would get a premium price, followed by Tamil newspapers and then the used notebook papers. For old newspapers, the buyers would even come home and buy. For high-quality papers like The Hindu, they would pay by piece, as they were sure of the standard weight. I did not know while subscribing to The Hindu that people took into account the resale value. But I did know there were quite a few subscribers who would consider it to be sacrilege to dispose of old Hindu papers and would rather create *new* attic space to store the *old* paper!

Opposite to my house in the South bazaar, Palayamkottai was a grocery store. We could watch the operations of the store from our front room. It would be fascinating to see the way the grocer was using the newspaper to pack. He would pick one full sheet of paper and rotate it through his hand swiftly to make a conical shape with a huge slack at the top to use as a cover. He would pinch half an inch of the sharp portion at the bottom and fold it up to prevent any leak at the bottom. He would be standing in a pit. From the ceiling above a big balance would be hanging on one side and a huge ball of twine thread on the other. (In later years, while in Canada, whenever I saw gyros/shawarma hanging in Greek or Middle Eastern food stalls in the market, I was reminded of the twine ball hanging by the side of the grocer.) He would place the required weight on one pan of the balance and the item being bought on the other. Then, he would direct the customer to look up to see if the needle was in the middle, indicating the correct quantity. But even before the customer had lifted his head to look up, the grocer would swiftly pour the sugar or rice or whatever that was on the pan into the paper cone, give it a few taps to even up the contents, and close the lid. Using his other hand, he would then pull the twine and weave it around the side of the package, starting from the bottom to the top and back, then around the side a couple of times before tying the loose ends. The package would nicely settle as if it were in a net.

The grocer would not be interested in buying old notebook pages. My buyer was the sweet vendor. The first task for me was to go over the notebooks to see whether there were unused pages. The unused pages would be torn away and later stitched together to make a 'rough' notebook. Rough notebooks were all-purpose notebooks used at home to do additional math problems or answer practice tests.

Our notebooks used to be of either forty pages, one quire (96 pages), or two quires. It would be difficult to tear the unused pages easily from the two quire math notebooks that were typically bound ones. Gathering all the used pages, test and exam answer sheets that were on long sheets, I would march to the sweet vendor with my used papers and return home richer by about two rupees and some change. Of course, after receiving the money, it was customary to haggle for some free snacks, and the vendor would oblige with a small pocket of pakoras. That packet represented the mitigation of the seller's (my) regret or reduction of the consumer surplus (a notional surplus being the difference between the maximum price that one will be willing to pay and the actual price paid) to the sweet vendor.

Like me, several other students in the neighbourhood would also be clearing their exam papers and notebooks to various sweet vendors. Hence, when we bought mixture or pakora from those shops we would get a package deal-item to eat and a page to read. Just like the message in Bottle Hunters, we would be eager to read the page that came with the pakora. In rare occasions, we might get our own paper, of course well oiled. From time to time, we would get hilarious and interesting reads. A page from an essay of a student who had liberally used the movie song lyrics as ancient Tamil literature and another using the names of contemporary cricketers as contributors to Tamil literature would not be uncommon.

Better still was when an exam paper from my friend where he had answered Manila as the capital of Indonesia landed in my hand. My power index went up a couple of notches. At the same time, I uttered a prayer to Lord Ganesha to ensure that my exam papers did not fall into the hands of my friends.

The next major task that we faced prior to the opening of the school was selling our used books and looking for used ones for the new year. Excepting for the textbooks for languages, where the government had some control, the textbooks for other subjects were left to the schools' discretion. As our school had adopted books whose authors were from our own school or its affiliated college, there would not be major changes from year to year in the books adopted. Hence, there was a market for used books. The price one would get depended on how well-kept the book was. There was always a very fine balance. To keep the book in a pristine condition, if I had not opened the book at all, there would not be a halva celebration or a book available for resale!

During the year I was particular not to underline as much as possible. Underlining with a pen was an absolute 'no no.' Instead of underlining, I would have used parenthesis at the beginning and end of the important lines and placed a mark on the side, all with a lite pencil. Hence, when I wanted to buy used books for me, I hunted for pencil lovers. But with a brother who was one year senior to me in school, my necessity to hunt for used books was limited. I got hand-me-downs, and I had no say on their condition, but then I got them free of cost. If I ever tried to complain, I would be reminded of the proverb, "Do not try to inspect the teeth of the cow that you get free."

Buying used books was a downer in the sense that the outer edges of the pages would have gone brown, and the stitches would have gotten loose. To enhance the durability, we would bind the books. As a part of craft class in school, we had learnt the principles of binding, which helped my brother and me to bind our books. The instruments needed were a poking needle that had a wooden head, a hammer, and a pair of scissors. We would poke holes through the book at about a quarter, half, and three-fourths of the length, about half an inch away from the inner border. We would cut a piece of twine, thread it through the top and bottom hole at the back side, bring the ends to the top middle and make a cross to tighten and thread back the ends through the top and bottom holes . Pulling the ends firmly at each end, the thread would then be brought to the front through the middle hole, where a tight knot would be made. The loose ends of the twine would then be snipped. A piece of calico cloth would be glued to the spine of the book and the cover boards at the front and back. A major gross thing in that operation was the animal bone-based glue that we used, which would stink for a mile. Decorative marble paper would be stuck on the boards, and that would complete our end of the binding. We would take the bound books to the printing press nearby, where we would get the edges cut for a nominal charge. Once the dirty ends were gone, the book would look beautiful. But alas! It would not have the smell of a new book, thanks to the stink of the bone glue!

Old or new, Math books had a special treatment. The answers for the end of chapter problems would be provided at the end of the book. Our math teachers wanted those pages stitched together so that we could not see the answers. They never believed in reverse engineering, perhaps! But we had our own ways. We used to blow air between stitched pages to lift the page slightly and perform certain unique variations of 'sirsasana' to read the answers.

We had treated all books with great reverence as it was and still are considered a form of Goddess Saraswathi. Therefore, the thought of selling old books to the sweet vendor never arose in our minds. A whole lot of old books from our elementary school days onward were kept in a box in my lawyer brother's house where we grew up. There were always alternate books from yester years for any given subject in that box that provided a source for additional math problems to try out or practice test questions to be answered in our rough notebook.

My brother preserved those books even when he was moving from house to house. Even after several years past my college days, it was always a lovely experience to go over some of my high school books during my visit to my brother's place. I used to tell my school-going nephews, much to their annoyance, that the standards during my time were much higher. I would turn the pages in my math book and point out a particular problem and tell them that was a killer rider to the theorem and required special construction to prove. Thank God it was Chennai. If I were to do the same in Canada, the kid would have called social service complaining torture! Unfortunately, during one of the flooding in Velachery Chennai, water entered the first floor of my brother's house and swept away the boxes of books. More than the loss of the fridge and the TV, he felt devastated that old books that his brothers had kept with him for safekeeping got lost.

In my college years, I never had textbooks for a number of subjects. Our professors devoted half the class time to dictate notes and that formed our study material supplemented by a few library books on loan for a short time period. The professors' notes were perhaps what they had taken down from their professor. The only textbook I had during my B.Com days was an accounting book by an English author, J.R. Batliboi. It was expensive and was not available in bookstores in Tirunelveli. My fifth brother, who was working in Chennai with an electrical manufacturer, took a trip to the famous Higginbothams to get the book. The book was priced in British Pounds, and he shelled out almost half his pay. It was ironic that I had my introduction to bookkeeping in Pound Shilling and Pence two decades after our independence.

All these childhood experiences created a great reverence for textbooks. While working at the University of New Brunswick in Canada, I used to receive complimentary copies of several textbooks from different publishers. I could never gather myself to throw any of them in the recycle box, even after receiving the next editions. For the first few years, I used to retrieve textbooks from recycle bins thrown by other colleagues. With the help of my colleague from Ghana we used to ship old books to African universities. After some years, the operation stopped as the universities could procure the latest editions reasonably cheaply in their countries under some aid arrangements.

Getting back to my school days, a week or so prior to school reopening, we would start buying notebooks for the school year. The school would sell in their depot notebooks with the name and emblem of the school. Those notebooks were more expensive than what we could get in the stationary stores. In our household, as a rule, we were not buying from the school depot. The only notebook that was bought from the school was the one used for English composition. The reason was that we had to submit the composition assignments every other week for the teacher to correct. Further, the composition notes of all the students would be kept for inspection by the district board inspectors. Those notebooks would have been neatly covered with brown paper and a decorative label stuck on them to write our names.

We had a mandatory uniform policy for Mondays only. Every Monday there would be a general assembly that would be addressed by the Head Master. They had specifications of clothing for the Blue shorts and white shirt uniform. It had to be made by Binny Textiles with some four-digit number added to the product specification. Our school had grades six to eleven, and there were six to seven sections in each grade and forty to fifty students in each class. There would be around ten to fifteen percent attrition in each class due to failing and moving out students. Overall, there would be more than fifteen hundred students enrolled in the school. That gave me immunity in getting generic blue shorts that were a lot cheaper.

The first day of school reopening would have a lot of buzz. Looking for the section and classroom assigned would take a good amount of time. By then, we would have figured out how many of our close friends were in the same section and had jointly worked out a seating strategy. During the day, we would find out who would teach what subject to us. All that excitement would be punctured when the English teacher came up with the first assignment for the composition, "Write an essay on your summer vacation-2 pages. Due in one week."

When my friends were thinking of writing about the cities they had visited, I thought I did not have a problem. I could say I was preparing for getting back to school and the essay was ready!

Later, When I moved to Canada, I was looking forward to my daughter's back to school days. I imagined the different notebooks, the brown paper cover, and the colourful labels that I could get her. I was willing to get her new textbooks and see the smile that they would bring to her face. When she brought home the list of school supplies and book to be bought. I was very disappointed. There were no notebooks or books to be bought. Instead, several Duo-tangs and loose-leaf ruled sheets with pre-punched holes were the only requirements. For each subject, she used different coloured Duo-tang, and she wrote on loose sheets and then filed them. The school supplied the textbooks. The teacher used to keep on his/her shelf enough copies of the book. Each student picked up a copy during class time and returned the same at the end of the class. The copy a student might get to use on a given day might not be the same copy received on an earlier date. Only if there was any homework, the student took a copy of the book home. But the homework was hardly from the book. Mostly the homework was some project that did not need the textbook. Hence, I had not seen her textbook at all until she entered the university.

I volunteered to go with her to the university bookstore. She bought a book on Physiology. It was so heavy that when I received it from the cashier, I almost sat down. I wondered how she was going to carry such books and walk, especially as she had never carried books during her school days. She said, as a matter of fact, "Dad, do not worry. This book is for the course of two terms, and there are four different segments. I will just tear the book into four and take only the segment needed." Hearing that, I was shocked and chided her as to how she could think of tearing of a new book, that too an expensive one. She showed me the cover of the book that had a picture of the spine and backbones and asked, "You want the book intact or my backbone?" When I had a closer look at the book, I could figure out from my binding knowledge that it had four independent segments bound together, and a proper dismantling could keep each part intact, albeit without a cover. I did not have a logical answer as to why the book could not be orderly dismantled. But still, I could not come to terms with tearing the book into four pieces. Finally, her suggestion that she would carry each segment inside a nice project folder gave me some peace of mind as the book pages would not be carried naked along with the folders. She bought a bunch of pink highlighter indicating that would show well with the colour of the pages in the book. I almost fainted, chanting pencil, pencil, pencil, please!

Now, I started liking e-books. I could undo highlighting!

Chapter 5 From Pencil To Pens: An Attempt to Ink

Being allowed to use a pen in the school represented a major milestone in a number of dimensions. We were allowed to use the pen in grade six, which implied the end of the elementary school and the beginning of the high school. Unlike the pencil, the pen had several moving parts. Learning to disassemble, assemble, and maintain the pen in good condition made me think I was an engineer (well, mechanic, at the very least). Further, things written by pen could not easily be erased. That indicated the confidence placed by elders in our ability and equally the responsibility thrust on us to be careful.

On Sunday mornings, after an oil bath, a good amount of time was spent attending to the pen. In a way, I could say I was a pen pal on Sundays. The operation would start with gathering the accessories needed. Initially, I would start with a mug full of water and an old torn 'banian' with ink stains from earlier uses. In order to be commissioned for such a use the banian should have at least a couple of holes around the sleeves or armpits and the seams giving up around the neck.

The task of separating the body and the neck of the pen would not be easy due to a couple of reasons. The grip portion would be invariably slippery, and the threads at the bottom of the neck screwing into the body would have accumulated quite an amount of muck. The ink, though reasonably fluid while being filled, would start leaving some small particles at the bottom as days passed by. These particles would have the same effect of clogging the flow as that of bad cholesterol in the blood stream. After opening the body of the pen, a quick look at the inside would give a fair estimate of the amount of ink left inside. If the quantity was negligible, I would simply drop the body in the mug with water. If there was a reasonable quantity, then I would pour it gently into the ink bottle. I would place the body of the pen in a slanting manner so that the residual particles did not get into the bottle.

The body of the pen would gently start sinking into the mug. As the barrel went down, the ink in would become thin and start floating, making patterns on the top. We could see the shape of Sri Lanka turning into Australia and soon an archipelago of islands. As the body got in, I would be yanking the feeder and nib from the neck. The feeder with several fins would look like a small fish stripped off its flesh. As the name indicated, it would feed ink from the body to the nib in a controlled manner. But, from time to time, it would have role ambiguity and feed the body with tiny paper particles. If we pressed the nib hard as if it was a plough, or if we used pen on unbleached paper used for our rough notebooks, it would result in small pieces of paper getting stuck in the feeder. Soaking in ink for a day or two, those tiny pieces of paper would disintegrate and move downwards into the barrel. It was like the blood-brain barrier getting breached.

Nib and the feeder could quickly be washed and drained. The threads in the neck would require extra rinsing and wiping to get small particles off it. The barrel might require some vigorous shaking to get the water out. To get the body completely dry I would twist the banian cloth and push it in all the way in, pulling and repeating that for a few times, just like a mother trying to get the water out of the ears of a toddler after a bath. Most of the time I would just wash and dry the cap. Occasionally, I would separate the clip and the cap so that the cap could get a thorough wash.

The inkbottle used to be on the window sill. We used to buy Brill brand of ink. Every time we bought ink, we would get a few labels free of cost from the shopkeeper. These would come in handy during back-to-school time. Once the parts were dry and ready, the pen would be assembled. I would fill the body with ink using an ink filler. Operating an ink filler was a fun activity in itself. I would squeeze the bulb at the top of the filler as much as possible to suck the ink from the bottle. Then, I would gently release drop by drop, counting the number of drops. I would try to squeeze harder the next time to increase the number of drops.

The problem with the filler was that during summer months, the rubber bulb would have stretched in the heat, and squeezing it would be messy. As I grew older, to show off my steady hand, I would just tilt the bottle at an angle and pour the ink straight into the barrel. As a safety net, the banian would be placed on the floor to catch any spill. A couple of my friends whose dads had businesses in Colombo in Sri Lanka had imported self-inking pens. Those pens had a thin plastic tube inside the body and a window on the body. One could squeeze the tube through the window. Keeping the pen upside down with the nib inside the bottle, squeezing, and releasing the tube would fill the ink in the tube.

My father had a beautiful pen with a pattern of golden yellow and green leaves throughout the body. The clip and the ring on the cap were golden in colour. The clip would look like a cross between a quarter musical note in a music sheet and a miniature golf club. On the body, he had his initials M.A.G   for Mannarkoil A. GopalaIaiyengar engraved. He carried the pen clipped to his shirt pocket. While writing, he always held the pen with his thumb and middle finger only, with the index finger lifted up. Whether he had a neurological issue or the index finger had the muscle memory only to pick up the 'chuna' the slaked lime for his betel leaf chewing, I did not know. Maybe he never wanted the stain of the chuna on his beautiful pen.

I got my first pen when I was going to school in Palayamkottai. My father got that for me. It was brown in colour and on the side had the name, 'Crest'. That was not any big brand-name pen like Pilot. In about years' time, my father became bedridden. Considering the space and domestic work support available, my parents decided to move to Mannarkoil, our village, for his treatment. Our family doctor from Ambasamudram was attending him daily. I, along with two of my school/college-going brothers and a sister, stayed with our lawyer brother, who was working in Palyamkottai. We used to visit our village during the weekend. Just a day before one of those visits, I lost my pen at school. But I did not tell anyone. My brother in my village found out that I was not in my element and wanted to know what was bothering me. I told him that I had lost the pen that Dad had got for me. In an hour's time, he took me to the store in the neighboring town and got me the exact same colour Crest pen. None of my other brothers or sisters noticed that I had a different pen. In a couple of years, the pen developed some leaks due to frequent falls, and I moved on.

A lot of us used to keep the pen cap stuck on the bottom of the pen while writing. That would give an extra length to hold and maneuver the pen. In addition, that habit would eliminate the possibility of the cap being buried in a messy desk. I belonged to those who would not place the cap at the end. This is because my habit of running around with the pen in my pocket and dropping the school bag that had the pen with a thud would result in some ink getting into the cap of the pen. Keeping the cap at the end of the body while writing would then make the body messy to hold. I used to take the cap off and put it horizontally in my pocket when the pen was in use.

There used to be a common phenomenon in the post office/bank line ups. A good number of the customers would not bring a pen, and the counter clerk would not provide one when needed. If the customers had filled up the forms properly things would move on smoothly. But invariably there would always be instances where a customer had not filled in the PIN code or another not signed the money order or the deposit voucher and the like. The clerk would ask them to fill in the needed item, and if they did not have a pen to finish the job then and there, they would get out of the line and allow the next person to be serviced, with the understanding that when they came back, they would be ahead of others. This set of people who forgot to fill the forms properly and forgot to bring a pen had excellent environmental scanning skill. As they stood in line, they would make a quick glance at people who had pens clipped to their pockets. The moment the counter clerk asked them to fill in something or the other, they would extend their hand to the identified target and ask, "Sir, may I borrow your pen for a second?"

I call such customers pen-pinchers. To be honest, even though the request would have a "Please," their hand stretch would almost reach into your pocket to take the pen. As if in a trance, the owner of the pen, I call them the donor, would hand over the pen immediately. It would appear like the unwritten smoker's etiquette wherein a person with a lighter visible in the pocket was expected to offer light when demanded by another smoker. The major difference being in the case of the lighter was that the owner never parted with the lighter.

After parting with the pen, the owner would be like a secret service agent-his eyes focusing on the pincher. As the pincher walked around in search of a counter space to work, the owner would mentally be registering the movements--two o' clock, five o'clock etc. That was when the owner would start getting panicky as he had to a turn to keep an eye on the pincher, and the person standing behind him would not like the face-to-face encounter of the person in front. Adding insult to injury, the person behind would even ask, "Are you getting out? The line is moving." Realizing the line was moving, the owner would pray he would get the pen and could start moving. Lo and behold, he would notice that he had left some items unfilled in his own form and would need a pen. That is when he would start desperately to scan the pockets of the people behind. In these situations, my habit of removing the cap and handing only the body to the pen-pincher was a guarantee for the safe return of my pen. Having an uncapped fountain pen in the pocket and walking away would be a recipe for disaster for the pincher.

With the arrival of ballpoint pens, the post offices and banks were "generous" in providing a ballpoint penrefill sans the body. That would be tied with a string and hung by the side of the counter. It would look like the rope with a slow-burning ember hanging by a pole in a cigarette shop. The only difference was the smoker was sure of getting the cigarette lit with the rope, whereas making the ballpoint refill work was not a certainty.

When ballpoint pens started coming up in the market, there was a lot of resistance from schools. They were not allowed for examinations, cursive handwriting classes, and composition assignments that were subject to inspection by the district board authorities. The structure of the ballpoint pen is different from the fountain pen. The ballpoint pen works by the movement of a small ball that was held tight enough by a socket not to fall, and loose enough to rotate freely at the top of the refill. The ball has a small hole at the top and bottom. The bottom hole has the ink, and the top, while rotated against the paper, disposed of the ink to create the writing. The body to grip the pen has a conic end. A small spring slid through the body rest at the end of the conic structure, and the refill is inserted through the spring. The spring and a thrust device at the cap, through a click or rotation, facilitate the ball to be in and out of the cone.

The ink in the refill is oil-based and that would perhaps qualify the user to be called a budding oil painter! The refills that we used to get were not of top-notch quality and would get frequent cardiac arrests. We would open up the cap and blow warm air through the bottom of the refill. That mouth-to-mouth resurrection would work sometimes. An alternate treatment was nose rubbing. We would scratch the tip of the pen vigorously on a sheet of paper, better still on the rough back cover of our math notebook, to get the flow going. We would have a pack of refills ready to replace when the ink of one was gone. We did not use pens with cartridges. What we used were inexpensive plastic tubes, and the level of ink could be easily seen.

Changing the refill sometimes could result in a missile attack. While pushing the refill through the spring, if we had applied extra pressure, the refill along with the spring would pop out. Finding the gray-coloured spring that fell on a cement floor would not be easy. Invariably, the spring would find a safety nook under the desk. But then we had a yellow rectangular box where all the spare parts retrieved from other old pens such as fountain pen neck, feeder, nibs, caps, springs, washers for the cap, and other knickknacks would be kept. The box had originally come with the aromatic LG brand asafetida inside, and became a knickknack box after the contents were used. But the aroma lingered in the box for a long time, giving our ballpoint pens an aromatic zing!

After my B.Com, I moved to Chennai and joined M/s S. Viswanathan, an audit firm, as an articled clerk aspiring to become a chartered accountant. There were about twenty or so of us at various stages of articled assistantship. Our assignments could be with different clients spread all over the city. But on Monday morning, we all would report to the main office located in George Town (G.T), the busy part of Chennai. That was when we would give a brief verbal report of the progress of our work, collect our travel allowance, and replenish our supply of audit pencils. Before heading to our audit sites, we would try to have lunch in the G.T. area, as there were a number of good restaurants. Usually, one group would move towards Palimar, an air-conditioned restaurant where food would be served on a banana leaf, and another to its non-air-conditioned version, Sri Krishna restaurant. A few of us would sometimes decide to have lunch at Ambi's café. The reason for the choice was that on Mondays, cricketer Venkataraghavan used to have lunch there and one could say hello to him.

Once, as I was walking on the Armenian street in the GT area, I saw the showroom of the Pilot Pen Company. My eyes popped. After my lunch I rushed to the showroom and got myself a brown Pilot pen with a golden clip. I was thrilled with my purchase. I used the pen for a long time.

When I went to Canada to work at the University of New Brunswick, I found that pencils were more in use at the university. Students were allowed to use pencils even for their exams and that was so different for me, coming from a place where even ballpoint pens were not allowed in the exam. I took to the pencil like a fish to the water. Given my terrible handwriting, it did not matter to my secretaries whether my manuscripts for typing were written with pencil or pen. Well, I could say I treated them with nice pencil sketches rather than ugly oil paintings!

When I retired, among other things, one of my gifts was a pair of Sheaffer pens--a fountain pen, and a cartridge ballpoint pen--nicely packed on a red velvet bedding in a decorative box. Given the prevalence of electronic mediums of communication, I did not find a good opportunity to open the box and use the pens. The only appropriate occasion where I could have used that pen was perhaps to sign the thank you note. But I used a black-inked Sharpie. While thinking of all those who played a role in my development, I remember my elementary school teacher, Gnaththamma. Though she had wished and hoped that I would become a Collector and sign in green ink (only gazetted government officers were authorized to sign in green ink in India), I was sure she, along with my parents, who lived in opposite each other, gave me a nod of approval for the profession I chose.

Chapter 6 Post Office Experience-from a Local Village to a Foreign Village

On one of my visits to my village, Mannarkoil, I found out that it had a branch post office affiliated to Ambasamudram (the taluk headquarters. Ambai for short) post office. Until then, there used to be a mailbox at Mr. Krishnamoorthi's house at the east end of the street, where he was an authorized agent to sell stamps. To my delight, the new sub-postmaster was none other than the husband of my aunt living opposite my house. He had retired a few months earlier after teaching in the primary school for over three decades.

The front hall in the east side extension of my aunt's residence was the post office. It was at a higher level than their residence. It had grills painted green. The drop-down bamboo curtain was hardly drawn. Hence, everything was visible from the street. He had a small desk and in its drawers, he had all the office stuff. That included the all-important seal, a cute small-pan balance, pieces of 'arakku,' the red-coloured sealing wax stick, and a small spirit-fueled burner of the size of an ink bottle.

'Athimber,' which is what we call the paternal aunt's husband, was always seen in a crisp white dhoti and a folded towel on the shoulder that could be unfolded and used to cover his upper body when needed. Unlike in Bengal, where the dhoti is worn with legs parted, the typical dhoti worn in Tamil Nadu was half as long, and wrapped around the waist, covering both legs together. Typically, the left side would be a little bit elevated, creating a pouch at the top and making the movements of the legs easier. Somehow, it would sit well on the hip without any belt. It was rumoured that anthropologists had undertaken research on the special shape of the hip bone of the Dravidian male that made it possible to wear a dhoti.

One could characterize the dhoti as an unstitched white lungi with a coloured border. The border is called 'karai' in Tamil and typically would be black, green or red. Dhoti with zari border was expensive and would be worn on special occasions. In the late '50s and early '60s, the border of a dhoti had become a medium of expressing one's political party affiliation. A black and red border denoting a member of DMK, and the same colour with the face of Annadurai in between the colours denoted ADMK members. In fact, the expression "Karai Veshti" –bordered dhoti -started having a special meaning. Over time, a tri-colour bordered dhotis also started appearing. Let me not digress.

Couple of other things that defined Athimber's identity were a tiny snuff box in the pouch of the dhoti and a bronze 'kooja' (water jug) by his side filled with hot water. He always had a scratchy throat, and he used to take a sip of hot water from the kooja every now and then to soothe it. He was very professional in maintaining the post office.

The post office had limited working hours. He would get ready around 11 a.m.or so and set things ready. The post office, in addition to handling sale of postcards, envelopes and stamps, had the facility to send and receive money orders. It used to be fun for us to get into his office and watch the activities. One needed to be silent. Otherwise, we would be chased out. Major activity would start when Raman, the postman, arrived from Ambai. Local people calibrated his arrival time to the timing of the town bus. Once the eastbound bus had left, Raman could be expected any moment.

Raman would bring the incoming mail in a long khaki string bag. He also brought a leather purse of the size of a cycle seat, tied and closed with molten arakku carrying the seal of the Ambai office. Inside that purse, were all the secured things. That included cash, stamps and any other confidential documents. Upon arrival, he would hand over the purse to the postmaster who, after verifying the seal was intact, would open it. Raaman would empty the mail sack and start sorting out the incoming mail.

There was an interesting job that would be given to the eagerly waiting kids, namely the date stamping of the mail. The initial task was setting the date. That would be in the middle part of the metal seal, whereas the outer circle had the location engraved. The moving of the dates requires fine adjustments of the wheel of dates that looked like a cogwheel. The next task was inking of the pad. Once that was done, one could stamp away to glory. Chuck, chuck, chuck... the noise of fast stamping would reverberate through the hall. The rubber stamp could be placed at the back or front of the mail, wherever we found space. On the other hand, for the outgoing mail, one needed to cancel the stamps. Hence, it had to be on the stamp but not on the face of the person on the stamp. The cancellation etiquette demanded that one did not deface the leaders on the stamp.

The persons expecting money orders would be waiting outside. Those who could not sign would have to place the LTI (left-hand thumb impression). The ink pad would be open for them to roll their thumb. For such persons, a witness was needed. Time to time, we were given the privilege of signing as witnesses. On those occasions, we were thrilled to be very important people. There was another set of people who could sign, but wrongly. I remember one of our servants, whose name was Gopalan. (Incidentally, the name Gopalan was so common in our village that one can find a Gopalan or its derivative in every other household. This was because the name of the local deity is Raja Gopalan.). But he signed as Kevalam (கேவலம்), meaning shame. Athimber would be aghast and lament because Gopalan was his student. At the same time, he was happy that Gopalan was making an attempt to write, and that would mean a lot to the next generation. The story about Gopalan was that he attended school only on the days when milk was distributed. For the rest of the days, he tended to his father's goats.

I do remember, even now, that in my school there used to be a pile of bags of evaporated milk powder with USAID stamps on the bag. In the school kitchen they used to make hot milk and provide the same for the mid-day meal scheme students. Though I was not part of the program, we used to get a spoon of the milk powder to taste. The sweet powder, unfortunately would become a paste and get stuck onto the upper palette. The tongue would have a job for the next ten minutes to dislodge the paste, thus making the net energy gain zero!

By the time the postman distributed the local mail, the outgoing mail would be ready for him to take. The leather purse would be stuffed with outgoing money order forms, cash, and confidential response mail. The purse would be closed with molten arakku, and the seal on top of it would complete the job. Once Raman left the office, Athimber would meticulously tally the stamp account, put the weighing balance and the seal in the drawer and close the office. That sub-post office was an institution in itself.

The post office experience in Palayamkottai, the bigger town where I had my school and college education, was very different. We were initially living in Pudupettai Street. It was a coincidence that a branch post office was next door. But in a couple of years, we moved to South Bazaar. South Bazaar as the very name indicated, was a major shopping street. The bazaar street /road was almost a mile long, running east-west.

At the west end was the Ganesh Temple. The temple was located on the outer wall of a fort. The word for 'fort' in Tamil is 'kottai.' The Palayakara rulers might have used the fort for administrative purposes and hence, the name of the town. The fort was almost in ruins. There were steps leading to the flat surface where a flag pole with the tricolour flag stood tall and majestic.

The east end had St.Anthony's church and a primary school for boys on one side, as well as The Seven Dollars Convent on the other side, offering primary education in English medium. The fact that the street started with a temple and ended in a church showed the diversity of the place. The postman would start his beat from the east end, and it would take more than an hour to reach our house, which was located at the west end, a block away from the fort. In the summer holidays, we would make it a routine to catch the mailman at the post office itself. That was not done with any sinister motive to smuggle progress reports from school. It was simply an excuse to get out of the house and escape from other chores.

The post office was about half a mile away from my house on the way to my school. The mail-sorting room could be viewed from outside through an open door. Mails that arrived from various locations would be piled in a canvas bin. The sorters would pick up a handful, look at the name of the street and throw the mail in the appropriate cubby hole. Their pick-look-throw movements were fascinating. Their head-turning downwards while picking up the letter, and going up for aiming at the cubbyhole and throwing the letter would look like a choreographed dance movement. And the letters flying from their hand into the cubby holes would look like shooting stars.

 After the sorters had finished their work, mailmen would collect the ones they needed to distribute from their cubby holes. There were about twenty or so mailmen covering various wards. Before they sat down to arrange the letters, they would give a glance at the eagerly waiting people like me and would make eye contact. Around a huge rectangular desk, they would sit and start arranging their mails busily. Each person had his own algorithm. My mailman would pick a handful at a time and give them a tap so that they stayed steady in his left hand. He would then flip through the mail and place them in order. That would give him a handful of arranged items. He would start with another batch and do the same and finally merge the arranged handfuls altogether. (On reading this now, my thought is that colleagues in the Operations Research Group might have written a couple of papers on whether the mailman's algorithm was polynomially bounded or not.)

Once all the mail carriers had finished their arranging, they reported to their supervisor to finish some paperwork. On their way out, they would be greeted by eagerly waiting residents like me on both sides of the door. We would be like the anxiously waiting drivers at an arrival gate of an airport sent by their bosses and waiting to receive unknown guests, except that there was no need for us to hold a placard. All the carriers used bicycles and they would be marching to the cycle stand. But prior to that, they would stop under the shade of the big tree and dispose of the waiting clients. I would yell, "31 South Bazaar," to which he would say," I know, and hand over the mail, if any, to me." Occasionally, he would say, "There is a registered mail and I will deliver at home." As the delivery of such letters needed signed acknowledgement of the addressee, he would not hand it to me.

One of the letters that we used to eagerly wait for was from my brother Raj (number four of seven boys where I was number seven), who had gone to Sheffield, England on a post-doctoral fellowship. He used to write regularly to my mother. In the initial days, he used to send an aerogram similar to our inland letter, except that it was longer and had three folds. The top fold had flaps on all three sides. The bottom third would be folded on to the middle and together they would be folded to the top. Then the three flaps on the top fold would be used to seal the aerogram. Opening the aerogram was an art. There would be clear instructions, but executing them was not easy. Invariably, by habit, we would open the top fold without opening the sides, and the aerogram would open like a harmonium. Our attempt to use a letter-opener often ended up in making three pieces of the letter. Reading the mail when the third fold got stuck in the middle would be an effort in itself-- turning it back and forth and up and down. Forcibly taking the stuck piece off would result in one line in the letter mangled with the bottom of the pulled piece. Lo and behold, that might be an important line. Furthermore, to get the full worth of the aerogram, my brother would scribble some messages (the P.S. part) on the side flaps that would be totally unreadable. Apart from the fact that the struggle of opening aerograms did not contribute to my immediate elder brother Rengan's stamp collection. Later on, when my brother felt a little more settled in England, he started to send airmail envelopes. However, the stamps from the UK were not pretty for a collector. But we got a lot of colourful stamps a few years later when my brother moved to Costa Rica.

Apart from staking out for our mail, a post office visit was needed when we had to send letters to my brother in England. As a policy, we used envelopes and not the aerogram equivalents. That implied we needed to weigh and assess the stamp charges. The envelope would be stuffed to the brim. Before weighing, the counter-assistant would want us to close the envelope so that we did not add any more after weighing (as if that was even feasible!).

Anyway, in a hurry, I would try to give a lick to the flap, and that was when I would feel the salty taste in my mouth. It would be the blood on the tongue from the paper cut. Well, my brother could certainly say he got a mail from a blood relative!

Sometimes, the lick alone would not do the job. Then one would resort to the indigenous glue kept at the side of the counter if one could tolerate the smell and the colour. The glue was made of boiled wheat flour kept in an aluminum cup. The intensity of the green colour and the hardness at the bottom could be used to estimate the age of the glue. There would be a stick but pulling the stick from the cup was a task in itself. The stick would get out such a lump of glue that it would be difficult to spread the gum with the stick. That was when I would pick a bit of the glue with the index finger and spread the same. But soon I realized that the finger had gone beyond the flap and got stuck to the already sticky countertop. Then, I would get alarmed as the envelope itself might get stuck, and pulling it off the counter would smudge the address. After all the ordeal I would be back to the stamp counter where the stamp vendor would declare the amount of stamps needed. As he flipped the pages to pick up the stamps, much to his annoyance, I would specify the various denominations of stamps that I wanted. My objective was to send as many different stamps as possible to my brother, who could, in turn, give them to collectors there. I never realized I was routinely exporting my fingerprints and DNA materials in terms of blood and saliva and some skin that got peeled off from my index finger with the glue.

My blood donation to the postal department also happened when I had to send registered mails with acknowledgment due. The small, thin white card for acknowledgement had to be attached to the envelope. That required poking a hole with a needle through the envelope and the card, and then tying them with a thread. The poke by the needle invariably overshot and pricked my fingertip to draw some blood. I always wondered how the acknowledgment card that was much thinner than a postal card, could manage the two-way journey.

From time to time, I would accompany my brother Rengan to the post office to get commemorative First Day Covers. I still remember one of the precious ones he bought, which was a cover released in memory of Mrs. Kamala Nehru. My brother was smart enough to carry that during his visit to the Parliament at a much later time and got the autograph of Indira Gandhi, the then-Prime Minister and daughter of Kamala Nehru, on that.

Later on, in 1982, I moved to Fredericton, Canada, to join the University of New Brunswick. Fredericton, with around forty thousand population was the capital of the province. In a couple of days after my arrival, I bought some envelopes and realized there was no bloodshed needed to close them. They had the peel and stick flaps. The store also had stamps, but I decided to get nice stamps of different denominations to stick on the mail and, hence, went to the local post office. A student from India who had been there for a couple of years was helping me find my feet in Fredericton. He took me to the downtown post office that was a block away from the legislative assembly building .

The post office looked compact with two nice counters and a glass top, and the total area looked much smaller than my village sub-post office. In addition, a good amount of the wall space was covered with mailboxes for rent, making the place cramped. There were about three people in front of me in the lineup. Within a few minutes, I got some pretty stamps, and as I was admiring them, my friend, who was waiting on the side, whispered asking if I knew who was at the head of the line. I was perplexed as to why I should know the person. Then, he mentioned that the person was the Premier of the province. (Premier of a province is equivalent to Chief Minister of a state in India). I could not believe what I heard. In Chennai where I came from, I would never expect the Chief Minister to stand in line in a post office and pay with his or her own money to buy stamps. Furthermore, roads surrounding the post office for half a mile would be blocked by police for public traffic if the Chief Minister were to go to the post office.

That was when I realized I had not moved to another village but to a foreign land!

PS. After five decades, the Gopalans of my village are still using thumb impressions to acknowledge receipts and payments. But the difference is they are not using thumb impression with the shame of illiteracy but doing that with the pride of tech savviness on their smart phone screens!

Chapter 7 Life cycle of learning to ride a cycle

Learning to ride a bicycle was an incredibly significant milestone while growing up. For someone who was short in height for his age, the waiting time was unbearable. Any time I raised the topic, a simple statement that I could not reach the pedal from the seat would settle it. Periodically, the cycle that was kept on its stand on the front verandah by the side of the wall would tempt me to check whether I could reach to the pedal. I would climb on to it carefully, placing my left leg on the connecting point of the crank arm and chain, squeeze my right leg over the top tube and, get to the seat and then get the right leg to the other side. Sitting on the seat, I would try to see whether I could get the pedal to go for a full round. To my dismay, I would find that when the left pedal went down, the right one did not rise to the level that I could push it with my right leg.

In my frustration, with the back of my left leg I would try to bring up the pedal that went down in a reverse motion. That was when the chain would come off the gear, and in panic, I would have liked to jump off the cycle and move away quietly to escape attention. Right then my big brother would appear from nowhere. Even if he did not see me on the cycle, he would know who did it.

After admonishing me on how unsafe it was for me to get on the cycle, he would take charge. Exploiting my guilty feelings, he would command me to get the old 'banian' cloth. He would move the cycle a little away from the wall and inspect the chain. Lifting the chain with the cloth, he would place it on the gear and try to move forward it by pushing the pedal with his hand. Once it was set, he would give a few fast pedals (rather hand pushes) to satisfy himself that things were all right. Seeing me standing idly, he would decide to oil the gear and ask me to get the oil can. The small round can would have a long-pointed spout to dispense oil. He would press the bottom of the can, and that would make a rhythmic sound as he poured a drop or two of the oil carefully onto the gear.

After a few such chain-tripping mishaps, to prevent further mischief from me, he suggested he would help me learn biking using a smaller bicycle that could be rented. I was thrilled at this suggestion. The next Sunday morning, I was all excited at the prospect of learning to ride a bike.

Around eight in the morning, we went to the cycle shop. The shop had only one small cycle and the demand for the same used to be high. The shop opened at eight, and we wanted to be early. The shopkeeper was just opening the shop. He brought all the big cycles for hire from inside his shop to the platform. During the daytime the entire pedestrian platform in front of his shop was used by him to park his cycles. I did not see a small bike and got a bit worried. But I then I spotted it inside the shop. Upon inquiry, he informed me that there seemed to be an air leak in the back tire, and he wanted to check it before renting it out. He informed me that it would take ten minutes and I could wait. My brother left me there and told me he would be back in fifteen minutes. He took the opportunity to visit his classmate at the end of the street.

The cycle shop owner had a helper, Ramu, who was probably a couple of years older than I was. Ramu brought a big aluminum shallow basin and filled it with water to about three-quarters level. The shopkeeper brought the cycle down, put it on its stand, and, with his hand, removed the tire and tube from the rim. After a quick glance at the tire to check whether there was any sharp thorn or needle on it, he handed over the tube to Ramu to check for a puncture. Ramu was thrilled to get a more meaningful job than simply sweeping the floor or bringing the tools and the like.

Giving me a glance with pride, he kind of signaled that I could watch. He sat down on a square stone that looked like his seat during the day and pulled the water basin in front of him. The tube had air but was not very firm. He picked up the tube and created a small segment of the tube about three inches long using his hands. Pushing down the tube on one side and holding it tight on the other side, he created a tight segment full of air. Then, he immersed that segment of the tube in the water and told me that he was watching for bubbles. Any time bubbles were seen, that would mean a puncture in that segment and air was leaking through the hole. Once a segment was cleared, he created an adjacent segment filled with air and repeated the process. Halfway through the tube, he located a punctured spot. He carefully drew a circle with chalk around the hole and checked the rest of the tube. He promptly informed the boss of his success in locating the puncture.

The shopkeeper brought a small orange-coloured rubber patch and a tube of vulcanizing glue. He roughed up the marked area a little bit and applied the glue. Placing that part of the tube on the stone seat, he stuck the patch and, gave it a good thrust and asked Ramu to wait for a minute for the patch to settle. After a minute, Ramu tested that part in the water to check whether there was any leak. To my relief, the patch had worked. Ramu then got busy drying the rest of the tube with the rag he had on his shoulder. The shopkeeper came back and put the tube and the tire back in the rim, then asked Ramu to get the pump.

Though Ramu could pump air, that would take more time. The shopkeeper, with his well-built body and height, could draw the piston all the way and give a good fill with every stroke. After giving a push test to the tire to check whether the air pressure was good, he took the pump off the valve and applied a saliva seal before screwing the cap of the valve. He then declared the cycle roadworthy. Ramu dusted the seat with his rag and gave me a good luck nod. My brother had arrived just then, and the shopkeeper noted his name in the register, looked at the alarm clock by the side of his cash box and declared 8.30. The cycle rent was charged hourly with a grace time of five minutes or so. If you missed that, you would have to pay for the next full hour.

We went to the V.O. Chidambaranar Memorial Stadium/Park. The place consisted of a park area where there were slides, seesaws, and swings on one side and a hockey ground on the other, with an administrative building and a large foyer to the building in the middle. It was in front of the foyer where the national flag used to be hoisted. Public meetings would be held on that ground, at which time dais and chairs would be placed in the foyer. There were concrete galleries on both sides for hockey game-watchers to sit and watch. For public meetings, chairs would be placed on the hockey field for people to sit. The hockey field would also be used for track and field events during sports days. Beyond the galleries on the left side was the area for the long jump, high jump and pole-vault. There was a big square pit, three-quarters of which was filled with beach sand. The runway to the jump area was a firm clay field nicely paved. That was the place chosen for our cycle class. Those who had learnt would move to the main field to have a few rounds of biking. In the evening, the pit area would be busy with people playing kabaddi.

The small cycle that we hired did not have a carrier at the back. Otherwise, my brother would have taken me as a pillion rider on the bike to the ground. After walking with the cycle for a few minutes, we reached the designated spot. While walking, I already got some instructions. "Look straight ahead while riding. Hold the handlebar tight. Do not use the right-side break," were some of the early instructions. Once in the ground ready to start the lessons, my brother tilted the cycle a little for me to get on to it. Once I sat on the seat, he held the cycle firm by holding the back of the seat and the handlebar. He then asked me to hold the handlebar and put the feet on the pedals. The left one was up, and the right one was down. Then he reassured me he would be holding the cycle by the back of the seat as I pedaled.

With all excitement I gave a push to the left pedal and realized it was not anywhere close to the ease with which I had pedaled the standing bike at home. And the right pedal was taking a free rotation before sticking to my foot. As I was trying to look down as to what was happening to the pedal, my handlebar started turning a little wobbly and that brought a stern warning from my brother:"Look straight ahead and hold the handlebar firm." In a minute or so, I got the hang of pedaling, but the handlebar was still not steady. That was when I got a push/pat on my middle back with a command," Sit erect." Sitting erect and with the assurance that my brother was holding the cycle, I started to pedal with a little bit of confidence, and the cycle moved nicely. As I was reaching the end of the path, my brother held the handlebar and helped me turn the cycle so I could go on the path again. I was more confident and went at a higher speed, making my brother run.

At the end of a round, we took a break. My brother used the time to show me the front and back brakes and warned me not to use the front brake ever, as it would tilt the balance badly. After nodding to all the theories, I was eager to get on to the bike. From talking to my friends as to how they had learnt, I knew that at some point, my brother would take his hands off. I mounted the bike with a lot of confidence and started pedaling. After going halfway through the path, I had a feeling that my brother had taken his hands off. Out of curiosity, I turned my head and found that my brother was a few feet away. As I turned my head, I lost my balance and fell to the ground with the cycle on me. I was hurting, but at the same time happy I was riding on my own. My brother lifted the cycle, inspected the scratch on my knee and declared that it was nothing. He reminded me sternly of the need to adhere to the first rule, namely, look straight ahead. That was when he told me the science behind hand-eye coordination and how important it was to look ahead and, not turn the head abruptly. After dusting up the bike he put me up and told me he would run by my side and I could bike without worrying about being on my own. He was constantly reminding me to hold steady and look ahead. At the end of the path, he helped me get down. By then, it was time for the cycle to be returned to the shop. My brother sent me home so that he could ride the bike to the shop. That was a memorable day.

After a couple more weekends and a cut in my knee, I had learnt the techniques of mounting and dismounting. But I could not use the cycle at home for practice as it was too tall. Periodically, I would beg my mother for money to rent a small bike so that I could have a few rounds. In due course, I learnt the "half pedal" mode of riding the big cycle. In that, I needed to get my right leg underneath the top bar to reach the pedal. That was a punishment, as my back would get squeezed between sides when the pedal goes up and down. Controlling the bicycle was not easy either. But the fun of riding a big cycle made me endure that pain. As I grew a little taller, I could graduate to a "three-fourth" pedal, where I would be standing and pedaling.

Even though I had learnt to ride a bike by the time I was in Grade nine, I never had a bike for myself until I was in the final year of my B. Com. That was the result of limited resources that were distributed using the family's economics principle of strict hierarchy. My immediate elder brother was just one year senior to me and I had to wait for him to graduate and move out of town for me to get a cycle.

But the cycle was available for off-school times when I needed to go the market to get vegetables or to get coffee beans at the India Coffee stores half a mile away from the house. Having the cycle to myself opened up the opportunity to make cycle trips with friends to nearby places. One such visit was to the nearby village Krishnapuram. An ancient temple with wonderful sculptures was in ruins, and the street in front of the temple was deserted. That evoked a mixed feeling of anger and sadness.

One of my hilarious cycle rides happened when I was working with the Union Bank of India. I was a probationary officer at Tirunelveli. Upon confirmation after one year, the bank duly gave me a Power of Attorney (PA) to act on their behalf. The copy of my signature and the PA number was circulated to all of our branches and other banks in town so that they would honour the cheques and demand drafts that I signed on behalf of the bank.

The immediate downside to the confirmation and approval of PA would be that you would soon be deputed to some remote 'one-man' branch. These branches were called one-man branches because there was one officer, one clerk and one subordinate staff running the branch. The officer could not go on leave unless someone from elsewhere took charge. The newly minted officers would be the scapegoats for such assignments. Immediately after the confirmation, I got the order to officiate as manager for a month at the Thirukarugavoor branch, as the manager there was availing himself of his much-awaited vacation. It was about an hour's bus ride from Tanjavur, the district headquarters, which was about two hundred miles from my place.

I reached Tanjavur , stayed in a hotel and took a bus to Thirukkarugavur the next morning. It took an hour or so. I reported to the branch with my order and the PA to be registered with the Tanjavur State Bank, where our bank had an account. The manager was thrilled to see me. He knew from his earlier experience that his vacation was not certain until he physically saw the reliever. The formalities of handover and takeover were completed within an hour, at which point he wished me good luck and left. The other two staff members were in disbelief that a thin twenty-two-year-old with curly hair was going to be their boss for a month.

Around lunch time I inquired the subordinate staff as to the whereabouts of the toilet. He gave me a key. It was not uncommon in small branches for the toilet to be outside of the building, and to prevent misuse by others, it would be under lock and key. After receiving the key, I asked him whether the toilet was behind the building. He pointed me to the cycle kept in the front and told me the key was for the cycle. I did not understand. Then he pointed outside. The branch was in the "bazaar," a little away from the residential area. Past the bazaar were farmlands. He pointed in the direction of the farmlands and told me:" Ride some distance, and wherever you feel comfortable, you can ease yourself, sir. No problem." I could not believe what I was hearing. I never knew that my cycle riding skill would come in handy in this way. And I was thankful that these rural branches were one 'man' branch.

After a few years with the bank, I changed my path and took to academics, which took me to Canada, where my daughter was born. I was all excited about the prospect of teaching her how to ride a bicycle. The first thing that I found out was there was no need to wait for years to start because cycles had adjustable seats. Unlike the fixed seat

I was used to in India, the seat of her cycle was removable. It was a saddle on a post that could be pushed into the hollow frame and clamped to the desired height. So her transition from tricycle to bicycle was quick. Actually, I should say from a tricycle, she got demoted to a cycle with four wheels. The bicycle had training wheels attached to each side of the tire that gave a broad base and kept the balance. As the cycle was of the height from which she could touch the ground, and it had four wheels, there was no fear of falling. I needed to help her only on the day we decided to take the training wheels off. I was disappointed. She missed the whole thrill of learning to mount and dismount from a bike where one could not reach the ground from the seat! Pedaling the bike with one leg to get the momentum and skillfully getting the other leg over the cycle without losing balance was a great skill I had, and I had no opportunity to show off.

Once she had grown out of the small adjustable bicycle, I was planning to get her a regular bicycle and decided to get one for myself too, so that we could bike together on the nice trails. When I went to the shop, all the cycles the shop had were with gears, and I had no idea of how to use the gears. Only in my late twenties did I know there were cycles with gears from the 'swing swing with the BSA cycle' ads. Even then, the focus was on the model and not on the cycle! When I looked at the chain case, there were coils and coils of chain link. The shopkeeper taught us the simple rules as to which gear to use while riding on down the slope and which ones to use while going up the hill. Nothing went into my brain as I had decided I was not going to use them. With our helmets, we both got set to ride our bikes home. That was my first cycle ride outside of India. As I sat on the bike I had a shock. The seat was hard. After getting used to a cushioned seat with springs underneath, the hard seat gave me a jolt. Riding on the trails was fun. The tires rolling on the crushed gravel of the trails made wonderful music. My house was about 200 meters from the end of the trail segment, but it was a downhill road. I got down from the bike and walked with my bike while my daughter was merrily operating the gear and riding down the hill.

The next day, I thought I would seek help from my colleague Dan, who rode every day to the office in his bike during the fall term. He lived in the outskirts about fifteen kilometers away up the hill. I was living within five kilometres of the university. I was hoping to get some idea about the gear system. I saw Dan coming down the hill quite fast with his body in a biker suit, hugging the top tube. That was intimidating enough. But after arriving at the cycle stand in front of our building, he stopped the bike, pulled out the front wheel, chained that to the rear wheel, and with a chain lock locked them together. He lifted the bike and pushed it into the slot of the cycle stand. If his speedy riding down the hill alone was sufficient to dissuade me, his act of pulling the wheel for locking erased any intention that I had to ride my bike to school. Looking at me, waiting and watching, he asked whether I needed something. I was tongue-tied and just said 'Nice cycle, Dan'. 'Thank you, Srini. I am going to the gym for a shower. "See you soon," he said and left. For some strange reason, the image of the cycle key that I got from the subordinate staff in Thirukarugavur flashed in my memory. I climbed up the stairs, reached the washroom, and told myself, "I do not need a cycle to come here!"

Chapter 8 Consumption: Urban Convenience Versus Rural Experience:

An Eureka Moment in a Marketing Class

I was sitting in the marketing class of Prof. Jain at IIM-A. He was trying to bring home the concept of consuming a product and having an experience. I was very sleepy thanks to an accounting assignment of tallying a trial balance that kept me awake till four o'clock in the morning. I vaguely registered a few words of the professor and started dozing off. Over the past few weeks, I had mastered the technique of keeping my eyes reasonably open while napping. That very useful yoga exercise was somehow never taught in the typical yoga classes where the guru would impress you with his ability to make his body into a pretzel. Of course, I had the advantage of thick eyeglasses that resembled the bottom of a soda bottle. It was not easy for some one to figure out whether my eyes were open or slightly closed unless they happened to see me from the side.

Knowing that the professor had the uncanny knack of catching the nappers, I tried to resist my sleepiness by forcing my eyes wide open. That gave me a good view of the professor sitting at the desk in his Khaadi kurta. The Kolhapur sandals were about to fall off his feet as he was dangling his feet. My resistance was short-lived, and I started taking off. The sight of the professor in his Khaadi kurta and the hand-crafted sandal took me to my visit several years ago to Kuralagam, in Chennai, the building where the Tamil Nadu handicrafts emporium was located.

Coming from a small town four hundred miles south of Chennai, I moved to the city to be an apprentice in the C.A firm, S.Viswanathan and company. The firm was named after the legendary founder and was situated in a building next to Kuralagam.   It was my first day, and Mr. Viswanathan, who was referred to reverently as Periyavar (elder/the boss), handed me a ledger. That had the accounts of the firm Dinroze Estates and he asked me to chart a trial balance. A senior apprentice who saw me walking to the desk with the ledger advised me to work with a pencil, as Periyavar did not like overwriting or crossing off numbers. Of course the trial balance did not tally at the first shot. Noting that the difference was divisible by nine, I thought it must be some miss-juxtaposition of digits while copying. With that confidence, I decided to take a break and entered the next building, Kuralagam.

Apart from Khaadi kurtas, hand-crafted sandals and other handicraft items, they had a stall selling pathaneer (பதநீர், neera, unfermented palm wine). Feeling nostalgic,

I bought a bottle of the refrigerated pathaneer and drank it with a straw.

As these thoughts were going on in my sleepy stage, I heard a few words from the professor that kind of shook me a bit. Again I heard something to the effect of experience. Finding it difficult to delineate whether the trial balance not tallying was in my assignment or in my first job, I dozed off again. But the taste of pathaneer was lingering. Somehow, it was not the same as what I used to have in my village. My mind wandered to the days I had spent in my village.

I used to visit my village during summer holidays, and one of the attractions was an early morning drink of pathaneer. Pathaneer is obtained by tapping a Palmyra type of palm tree . By the time the tapper, whose generic name was Nadaar, came to our street, his pot would be almost empty. Hence, I used to take an early morning walk along with my cousins who grew up in the village, to the parcel of land where the trees were.

The tapper used to carry a walking stick kind of a thing with a good recessed plank at the top like a hand rest. It would look like the stands that great rishis kept to put their hands on while in deep yoga. He would have a long, bending-at-ease bamboo pole balanced well in the recess. At each side of the pole, one could see earthen pots and other accessories. Sometimes, he carried the pole on his shoulder and the stick tucked under his arms.

As we used to go to the farmland early in the morning, we could observe his entire operation and that always fascinated me. Upon reaching the tree, he would put his pole down and keep the stick leaning toward the tree, making a right-angled triangle. His accessories included pots, knives, 'aruvaal,' (billhook machete), hydrated quicklime, filtering sieves, ropes and the like.

Palmyra trees are typically very tall, and the trunk very rough due to the stubs of branches that had fallen off over the years. Climbing the tree is an art. Our Naadar would take a rope twisted in the shape of eight and get his feet in it. That would be his hiking boot! He would pull out a chest protector made out of coconut fibre ropes. His dhoti would be tucked well above the knee like a sports brief. He would look like a Samurai warrior with a fifth of the mass. The thick leather belt around the waist would have hooks to carry a pot, knives and 'aruvaal.'

He would coat the inner part of a pot with hydrated quicklime. That would be a replacement pot for the one he had placed on top of the tree on one of his prior visits. The coating of quicklime was to prevent fermentation. Fermented pathaneer would be toddy. It was rumoured that in the evening shift, he might put an uncoated pot.

With his hiking gear and chest protector, he would start climbing. Walking up on the leaning stick, he would get to a squatting position, hugging the tree trunk tight. After a moment of surveillance and a prayer, he would stretch one hand all the way high and hold the trunk, followed by the other. And then he would move his chest up hugging the tree until the legs are fully stretched. He would then take a breath in a full-stretched position. It would appear as if he was seeking the blessings of all his ancestors up in the sky. Then, he would get into the squat stretch routine, climbing several feet each time until he reached the top. My mind wavered for a moment to imagine how Prof. Bhatnagar in the computer course would put it in a 'repeat until' subroutine format:

REPEAT

   SQUAT

      STRETCH

         BREATH

            HOP

UNTIL the tree top is reached.

Soon, my rapid eye movements (REM) brought me back to the tree. Once on top, Nadaar would squat comfortably in between branches of the tree. Looking up from beneath, it would not be easy to see him. It was the leaning stick and other accessories on the ground that would indicate his presence.

Pathaneer is tapped from the inflorescence embedded in the bark at the top of the Palmyra tree. He would inspect the barks to decide the right one to tap. With his sharp knife, he would make a few fine cuts at the tip of the bark and make a few targeted incisions for the sap to drip. He would then tie a pot around the branch in place to gather the sap, trim some dead flowers and leaves. The shavings would land in a little swirl, indicating that there was someone up on the tree. He would inspect the pots tied on earlier days and gather the liquids in a pot ready to bring it down with him.

Before climbing down, he might cut a bunch of fruits (called 'Nungu' in Tamil) that were ripe enough, and fell a branch whose fan-shaped fronds or leaves might be needed for the day. Because of the anticipated fall of stuff from above we would keep a safe distance from the tree. After securing all the pots, he would climb down in the same manner as he went up, hugging the tree. I made a mental note that the algorithm should end with 'until the ground is touched,' and that 'hop' should be replaced with 'slip down'.

Eagerly waiting for his landing, we would slowly approach him. He would get out of his hiking gear- I mean the toe ropes. put the pot down and remove his chest protector. In spite of the protector, there would be scratches on the chest, and over the years, a good part of his chest was scarred. The contrast of the scars and the stretched-out skin would appear as if he was walking with his chest x ray displayed.

Once settled he would acknowledge our presence and get ready to serve. Pathaneer is generally served in palm leaves. He would get a leaf from the branch he had felled and clean it up with his hands. The long leaves would have gathered some mushy stuff from the flowers. He would carefully push them out with his fingers. In fact, we would gather the mushy stuff to feed the peacock feathers that we had tucked in our book pages. It was believed that the mushy stuff would help the feather multiply inside our book. Aren't those innocent beliefs amazing?

He would shape the leaf like a boat by pushing the middle to create depth. That part of the mid rib of the leaf closer to the branch would be strong and form the head of the boat. The tail part would be weak and not jointed. He would tear a piece of the leaf at the end and tie it around the tail part to keep it firm. Drinking pathaneer from the palmyra leaf boat requires skill. He would give the boat in our hands and dip his measuring cup made of aluminum into the pot. In the pot one could see floaters consisting of flower buds and dead ants and other insects. At the bottom one could see the quicklime sediment. We would beg him to give us from the top and not to disturb the quicklime at the bottom to avoid the caustic taste of quicklime. Being a regular and early customer, he would oblige and pour the pathaneer through the filtering sieve into our leaf boat. Holding it steady I would ensure that the liquid was not flowing to the leaky tail end. Holding it still for a few moments would help the quicklime particles to settle down at the bottom. The filtered juice being colourless would simply reflect my eager face. The green tinge of the inside of the tender leaf would add a glow to my face. I could admire that sight for any length of time but then I was equally eager to   drink.

Bringing the leaf boat to the mouth and tilting it just enough without pouring the liquid on my shirt was not that easy. My cousins from the village would have finished their share in a jiffy and would take the role of my cheerleaders.

They would genuinely appreciate my decision not to bring a glass with me and try to drink it in the way they did. I would get instructions such as "Do not crush," "Left hand a little up," and the like. After gathering much courage, I would take the ship to my lip and have my first sip. Wow, that would be something. The clear, sweet drink would take you to a different place. Fresh from the tree, not mixed with the pathneer from other trees, and served in a boat-like thingy made from the green leaves of the same tree is some unique experience. Now I understand why some of my friends long for single malt stuff. After finishing the drink we would untie the tail end, fold the leaf and leave by the side of the tree for nature to take care of it in due course. And of course, the foamy mustache formed on the upper lip would be given a quick lick to extract the last bit of pathaneer. Then we would pay him, inquire of him as to what trees he would be climbing the next day and leave.

Between the taste of that and the one I had at Kuralagam, there was no comparison. One was an experience as if I was on top of the tree, and the other was consuming a product in the basement of the shop. That was my eureka moment. I found out that the distance between the consumption of a product and experience of witnessing the product being made specially for you to consume, is equal to the height of a Palmyra tree. Finding such a fundamental equation, I was about to shout eureka. Just then, Prof. Jain was having his customary walk through the isles and observed me from the side. With a grin because he had caught me inattentive, he posed the question   as to what I had got thus far in the class. Barely out of my trance, I told him 'I found that the difference between consumption and experience equal the height of a palm tree.' Hearing that, the whole class went into laughter. Not minding the laughter, I asserted that I could prove it and started narrating my two different instances of having pathaneer. That level of participation gave me a free ticket from class participation for the rest of the term. And that helped me to doze off in his class and come up with other inventions!

Chapter 9 Sir, Are you illiterate?

Indian Institute of Management Ahmedabad (IIMA), where I graduated from, is one of India's well-known business schools. It has a beautiful campus designed by the famous architect, Louis Kahn. It is a residential campus, and during the academic term, full of hustle and bustle. As the summer term is a work term for the students, only a few of the doctoral students used to be around the campus. The summer days in Ahmedabad are very hot, and the campus would look almost deserted. On the other hand, summer was a good term for doctoral students to get some work done, not due to the absence of other students. but simply because only the library and the computer centre used to be air-conditioned in my student days.

Forty-five years ago, I was a doctoral student at IIMA, spending the hot summer days on the campus preparing for my comprehensive examination. I was working on a problem of optimal scheduling of cash transfers across bank branches. The heat during the day used to be unbearable. My daily routine was to take shelter in the library after breakfast until the lunch hour. A mini-break during lunch hour included lunch in a mess and a walk to the 'paan-wala' (seller of betel leaf preparations) in front of the campus.

The paan-shop was a kind of boxed cart similar to the hot dog stands in front of downtown offices that I see now in Canada, but not motorized. The front side of the covered cart opened out as a table. Gopalbhai, the owner-operator, would sit on a bar stool inside the shop with all the ingredients to make a paan in front of him. Before he opened the shop, he would ensure that all the small, well-polished brass/copper cups full of things were in order, and fresh consignments of betel leaves of different varieties (Banarasai, Calcutti and the like) were well laid up in nice small buckets with water. He would cut a few old cigarette boxes into fine strips and keep them by the side of a chimney lamp at the inner corner of the table. The vast majority of his smoking customers bought one cigarette at a time and did not buy matches. They would pick up a strip, dip into the chimney lamp to get the fire, and light their cigarettes. With a bucket of water in front to dip his right hand in, and a towel on his shoulder to dry it, he would be ready for business after a few minutes of pooja.

In spite of its being on a mobile cart I never visualized the shop as a temporary establishment. Its permanence was brought about by a thatched roof extension in the front. That provided a shaded area for the customers to congregate and spend a few minutes chatting with Gopalbhai. It was customary to see people working on the road works and construction sites nearby squatting under the shaded area and taking a break enjoying their 'beedis' (indigenous cigarettes). Next to the shop was a fresh sugarcane juice vendor. In summer, people used to drink sugarcane juice to protect against dehydration. Due to the hot weather, the sugarcane looked so dry it was a miracle he could extract juice from it. The cane and some ginger would be crushed in a hand-operated mill, and the foamy fresh juice would be poured into a glass. Some of the customers would bring their glasses to the front of the paan shop to enjoy their drinks under the shade.

It was during one of my post-lunch time visits to Gopalbhai that I had my enlightening moment. There was another customer with him when I arrived. As he knew my preferences, there was no need for me to order, just some eye contact and his acknowledgement of my presence was enough. So I stayed back watching the road. An old lady was pulling a hand cart with a refrigerator to be delivered somewhere. She brought the cart to rest in front of the shop. I thought she was stopping to get a paan. She approached me and pulled a crumpled piece of paper tucked in a pouch of her colourful Rajasthani outfit and asked me in Hindi the directions tor the address written on the paper. I had a working knowledge of Hindi in terms of understanding the spoken language, and with difficulty, I could read Hindi script. I understood her concern; with such a heavy weight on a hot day, she did not want to travel far beyond her destination. The loader of the cart had given IIMA as a nearby landmark, but IIMA was located at the junction of two roads, and she needed to know the correct road to take for her destination.

As I opened the paper, I realized it was written in Gujarati. I had no clue as to what was written. My mother tongue is Tamil. My education was in Tamil and English Medium. Hindi was not taught, but I had a working knowledge of Hindi. I never felt the need to learn Gujarati, even though I had lived in Gujarat for a couple of years.

I was staring at the paper with an address while the old lady was eagerly waiting. Not only the letters, even the numbers were in the vernacular script. Unlike Tamil Nadu where I came from, in Gujarat they did not use Arabic numerals. Even in the city bus system. the Arabic numbers would only be indicated at the back. I never knew the number of the incoming bus but I always found out the number of the bus that I had missed! What appears like an eight in the Arabic is four in Gujarati. Hence, I never ventured reading Gujarati numbers. I apologetically told the cart lady n Hindi,"muje patha nahi," meaning 'I do not know.'

She was stunned by my answer and, with concern, asked, "Saab aap unpad hai?" "*Sir, are you illiterate?*" I was speechless. She was more than my mother's age, and she took one step further in her taunt by adding something to the effect of"You are well dressed but illiterate; you should be ashamed." It hit me like thunder, and yes, ashamed I was.

By that time, my paan was ready. I picked it up and walked back to the gates of one of the top schools of management, where only the cream of the cream got admitted. Little did anyone know that they had illiterates among them.

I suddenly realized that outside the gates, I had met one of the best teachers in my life. That was a day of enlightenment for me. My learning from that day has helped me a lot in my forty years of teaching career. I try to impart to my students the importance of contextual relevance.

If my knowledge cannot alleviate the pain of one in need, I am illiterate, or my knowledge is useless. I may be capable of solving a complex logistics problem to minimize the weight times the distance travelled of goods moved, but I could not help an old lady pulling a loaded cart on a hot day.

I walked away without answering her that day. But today, let me say this. "Lady, I was illiterate then and perhaps still am in some other contexts, and thank you."

Chapter 10 Chasing the Goal of Playing Hockey

The house we had rented at Pudupet South Street, Palayamkottai, was a portion of a bungalow in a compound belonging to a judge by the name of Bhairavan. The gated bungalow had a main entrance in the south street and a back entrance in the middle street. On opening the gate, one could see a big neem tree on the left, by the side of which there was a toilet and a cowshed. Municipal water tap and an open bathroom were on the right side. In a few yards were steps leading to a hexagonal wall about three feet high with a cement floor at the center, giving a stage-like appearance. In the middle of the floor, there was a lotus-shaped engraving that looked like the site of an aborted water fountain. We had rented the major portion of the bungalow consisting of three rooms on the ground floor and the upstairs. The property manager, who had four kids-- two sons and two daughters--occupied the backside of our third room and beyond. A young couple with a small kid occupied another portion of the main house that was by the side of an open verandah at the back of our portion. In addition, there were two outhouses in the compound rented out to two other families.

One side of the compound was walled whereas the other had some thorny shrubs between the boundary of the house and the backyard of the neighbour. In front of the outhouse and by the side of our house there was a big open space that was our playground. The property manager's son Jagdeesh, Sekhar my brother and myself, and a few kids from the neighbourhood used to play hockey on the ground. Sekhar had given me a junior size hockey stick that he had been using earlier. However, it required some repair. The stick was an assembly of two parts: the blade and the handle. The handle part had become loose. I had to take out the handle and refix it. That required melting animal bone-based glue (வஜ்ரம்) and applying it on the inside of the V-shaped opening in the blade and carefully inserting the handle and letting it dry. The collagen-based glue had such a terrible stink that I had to keep the stick in the cattle shed for a day. Once it got dried, to reinforce the binding and to absorb some shock, I had to wrap that part with some cloth tapes. The roll of tape that my sister had kept to use for her petticoat, came in handy. Once the wrapping was done, I had a stick to play hockey with.

The ground area was sufficient to hold about eight of us. We had a ball made of corkwood. Of course, we were barefoot players. The daily game would start after we returned from school and would come to an end when one of the following happened: A hit by the cork ball had made a bump of equal size on my ankle:, the thorn at the outer edge of the ground had stuck deep into my heel; or my brother and I were summoned by my sister for the evening prayer in front of the Diya, to be followed by supper. We lived in that house for two years, during which time I played hockey regularly. The blade of my stick being broad I could make a dead stop of the passes and move. I had also developed the skill of scooping the ball so that I could pass it to our team members quickly. As we moved away from this house to the South Bazaar house, the set of friends changed, and we played 'round race,' a local version akin to baseball.

In round race, we had four bases to run to score a run. There was an umpire who would bounce a tennis ball on the home base. We had to hit it with a stick or tennis racket, depending on how resourceful the group was. The fielders were allowed to throw the ball on the body of the runner to get the runner out, in addition to throwing the ball to the common before the runner reached the base. A catch also would get the person out. The innings would be over when there was no one left to hit the ball. Those who completed a run were considered alive and could hit again. Just like a home run in baseball, we had what we called a full run--when someone could round all four bases in one hit.

It was a very interesting game, and we used to play in the nearby playground. The major advantage of this game was that there was no need for individual gear. The tennis ball we would procure were from the tennis club near our school. They periodically disposed of their used balls.

Though I was not playing hockey I had kept my interest alive. Every year, there was a national level hockey tournament called Appa Memorial Tournament, named after the organizer's family. In our town. Lakshmi Mills Kovilpatti was one of the sponsors. The tournament attracted teams from all over India. Some of the big-name teams were ICF, Southern Railway Madras Engineering Group of the Army, Aligarh Muslim University, State Bank of India and the like. Our school, St. Xavier's High School, as well as the college, had very good hockey teams. Our school had won state-level school championships. The best feature of those wins was the headmaster praising the team in the school assembly and declaring that day a school holiday to celebrate the victory. My classmate Kumaresan, the captain of our school team, was a full back for the Tamil Nadu State-level Schoolboys' team.

Our college also had a very good team and had reached up to the semi-final of the Appa Tournament a few times, and that was huge given the level of competition. The centre forward for the college team at that time was one Vasant and he was the son of the organizer. Vasant was a tall and handsome lad. He used to look fresh even after an hour of play because he never ran all over the place. He would be there at the right place to receive the pass. He would dribble admirably for a few yards and score. He had a unique style both in his play and in his attire. He would wear his shirt with the middle portion of the collar lifted. Several students emulated that and we used to call that Vasant style.

I used to buy a season ticket for the tournament and watch the matches with my friends. We would attempt to shake hands with some stars after the match was over. Palayamkottai being four hundred miles south of Chennai, just fifty miles north of the southern tip of India, it was a big thing that players from far corners of the country visited the town. We had seen several players who were Olympic players or on the verge of becoming one. Apart from the player calibre, a variety of other things also got etched in my memory.

The first time I saw a player named Car, I could not reconcile that Car was really a name. All I knew at that time was that car meant pleasure car, the transport vehicle. Much later, I understood that it was one of the typical last names of English people, and he was an Anglo-Indian. Added to the name, what was incongruent was Car played for the railways. Car playing for railways? Another incident that I remember was with the State Bank team. Muneer Sait, the Olympian, who was at the goal. At the end of the match, a few of us went behind the goalpost to shake hands with him. He was busy getting out off the heavy goalie uniform. As he was pulling off his shirt, his sacred thread got jammed. It was an unexpected sight for us, and we could not control our giggles. First, we did not expect him to have a sacred thread as that was not our stereotypical image of a hockey player, and second the tussle he had in putting it back carefully appeared like slap stick comedy. He was extremely friendly and shook hands with all of us. Another fascinating sight for us was the way the players of the Sikh community tied their hair in place like a bun and played. Among the many players that we could watch, Cariappa of MEG and Govinda of AMU were super stars. Again, it was perplexing that a player with the name Govinda was playing for Aligarh Muslim University. I thought it would be a tit-for-tat if Aslam Sher Khan played for Banaras Hindu University!

When I was at the Indian Institute of Management, Ahmedabad, doing my doctoral program, I saw a notice one day. There was a call for the selection of hockey teams to play in the inter-dorm competition. They had names like Trojan, Ajax, Spartan etc., that were Greek to me anyway. I thought that given the popularity of cricket, hockey might not be the game of choice for many. Furthermore, at our school, the hockey players were not the ones aspiring for Engineering or Science degrees and by extension, most of the IIMA students, I thought, might not be interested in hockey. Hence, I thought I might get a chance to upgrade myself from 'a hockey player at one's own home ground' to a player for a team and that too with a foreign-sounding name.

With that thought, I went to check out the lawns opposite to Room 320, where the potential players were to assemble. I saw Srikanth Datar arriving with a bundle of hockey sticks, and G Natesh rushing towards his dorm telling Srikanth that he would get his cleats and join. The moment I heard the word cleats, I realized that they were into serious hockey and they were not planning for barefoot (नंगे पांव) hockey. With my shoe collection at that time being a dress shoe, a Kholapuri sandal and a pair of flip-flops, I quietly moved out of the place, realizing I was out of place.

When I moved to Canada, I did have a few pairs of sneakers. Hence I thought I could explore playing hockey as a pass time/exercise. I went to the sports goods shop and enquired about hockey sticks. They were showing me ice hockey sticks and helmets. When I indicated I was looking for a field hockey stick, the storeowner kind of looked at me and quipped, 'I suppose it is not for you, sir.' When I probed further, he indicated that field hockey was played only by girls in Canada.

That ended my hockey chase.

Recently, I saw in a group posting that 'India is having a hockey stick' economic recovery. I did not understand, as I have not heard a similar expression in Canada. Then I realized that it was the well-known J curve they were referring to. No wonder it is not called hockey stick recovery in Canada because hockey is played over slippery ice, and that is not the state in which they would like their economy to be in!

Chapter 11: Time to Bring Back Talk to Me Now (TTBBTTMN) Club

After my retirement I thought I should participate more in household chores and help my wife out. Beyond the routine task that I was already doing of collecting the garbage bags across bathrooms and kitchen, and getting them out for pick-up on the designated day, I was looking for an upgrade. After all I know a little bit of Maslow's hierarchy of needs. My self-actualization urge demanded that I do the laundry. But my wife would never allow me near the high-tech washer and dryer that we had bought. Every time I offered to do laundry, she would promptly say that it was all tricky, and I would mess it up. She would promptly remind me of the sweater she could not wear because a few years earlier, I had mistakenly put it in the dryer and shrunk it to the size of a knitted tea coaster. Somehow, I had never learnt to take the Fifth Amendment to the follow-up question of "Do you know how much it cost?" I honestly did not know, but hoping to ease the loss, I had given a low estimate. Pat came the reply. "I know you go for cheap sales in a departmental store. This one I bought in a boutique store," and the price she had quoted was about four times my estimate. Of course, I had the suspicion that the fudge factor in her estimate was high, but I did not dare to contest it at that time. From that time onwards, I always wanted to do laundry to impress her and redeem my self-worth in the field of choreology.

The new high-end electronic menu driven washer and dryer that we had bought increased my appetite to operate them. But I had a restraining order not to get near it. Thinking my wife was asleep one day, I started looking at the machine, and my fingers accidentally touched some button. As if it had been programmed by my wife it started beeping immediately. With her sharp ears, she figured out I was trying to fiddle with the washer. She responded immediately, "I told you not to go near the machine. If you break it, we need to change the chip, and that will cost more than a new machine. Let me see what you have done.: Nothing happened, no sweat," I replied, simultaneously bending down to read the scrolling words on the small plate. They were going at a rapid speed, and with my bifocals, it was not easy to read. The maximum speed I could handle was the CNN chyrons. The message on the plate was perhaps scrolling at double or triple the speed of the CNN chyrons. Whatever little I could read did not make any sense and that is when I realized I might have changed the menu to Spanish or German! My wife came down and pushed me away, saying she needed space and did not want me watching over her shoulder. In a second, she did something and the beep was gone. She told me she had cancelled the menu and showed me out of pity where the cancel button was. To test my skill, I tried to touch the cancel and, with my stubby fingers, touched something else, and the beep went on again. Like a firefighter, she quickly got to the cancel key. This machine had made a big dent in my self-worth, and I wanted an opportunity to redeem it.

When my wife had gone out on a shopping trip, I thought I would do the laundry and thus reduce her work on return. In addition, I wanted to really master the machine. There was a good amount of time before her return, and I had sufficient margin for a few mistakes now that I could locate the cancel button. After all, these machines are foolproofed.

Unlike my old machine, the new one had multiple slots in the soap area: one for soap, one for bleach and another for fabric softener. Luckily, the contrast in the print colour was helpful to identify which one was what. After filling the soap and loading the clothes, I carefully read the settings and pushed the delicate setting to be safe, as there were a few of my wife's outfits in the load. I learnt quickly that the buttons were feather touch, and when I pushed hard, they repeated the menu and started beeping. Further, my index finger was sprawling to more than one key. Immediately, I switched to my little finger. Finally, I managed to set the cycle, etc. and pushed the start button. I did not realize the first time that I needed to keep pressing it for three seconds, and there was a countdown. When it showed 'one' I took the finger off. Nothing worked. Then I did it again, and this time, I obeyed the instructions and held it for three seconds. The machine made a click, and there was the sound of a lock. I was reminded of the game show where the host asked the participant whether that was the final answer that could be locked in. I thought I had conquered.

Lo and behold, after a couple of spins it stopped and flashed an error message 'LF'. Ahah, I have come prepared this time, and looked up the online manual. That was the load factor (LF), and I might have to add more clothes. That was where perhaps my problems started. I ran upstairs and found a few more of my shirts and a couple of my wife's blouses on our closet floors. Quickly, I got them, filled the washer, and went through the drill. This time, the load cleared, and the wash went smoothly. I was having the thrill of my life when the machine announced the job done by gentle music.

Then, it was the time for the dryer. I remembered I should check the instructions carefully. Otherwise, I might get another tea coaster. Most of the items were drier-safe. Only in a few of the items I had some difficulty. One had pictorial instructions. The IKEA generation assumes everyone was pictorially literate. I could not figure out whether the picture meant line dry or it was a sign for a top-loading dryer. I was ready with the Google search and figured it out.

The next garment turned out to be trickier. The instruction tag was kind of crumpled. When I stretched it, there were instructions in five different languages, and as one would expect, the instructions in English were totally crumpled. Smartly, I pulled my iron box and ironed the creases out of the instruction tag. To my dismay the first instruction that became visible was Do Not Iron. I rushed to pull the plug and decided I would dry it outside.

The third outfit looked a bit expensive, and I did not want to fool around. There was no washing instructions tag. There was the brand name and some wiggly lines in a square. Since there was still some time before my wife's arrival, I thought I would call the outfit manufacturer. The customer service person was very receptive to my problem and told me that the issue could be resolved if I could upload the QR code. What in the world was a QR code, and how could I upload that was my question. The call center person was very happy to tell me that the company sells a companion washer dryer that will automatically read the QR code and sets the washer dryer settings for the outfit, and there was a special sale for them with a $2,000 discount. Without waiting for my response, he connected me to the sales section and put me on hold. Quickly, I disconnected and started googling.

I found a site that precisely addressed my issue. Of course, I had to register. Without asking further questions, it popped the message 'Male 60 Plus' and advertisements for reading glasses and denture gel were popping. I was impressed that visiting the site was like reading Tarot cards. I refused to get distracted as I had a job on hand. I soon found out that they had an app that I could download on my laptop. (Thank god it did not need a mobile.) I downloaded the app and showed the tag in front of it. It gave a message TTTO.

Puzzled with the message, I remembered the 'call a friend' option in gameshows. I had, by chance, met an old schoolmate last week who had studied computer science and made big in a software firm. It all happened when I was stealthily buying a white chocolate cookie in the coffee shop. He put his hand on my shoulder from behind and, pointing to my continuous glucose monitor patch, asked whether I was allowed to eat cookies. With the unexpected audit, I was shocked, and dropped the cookie on the tray to see who it was. Luckily, the cookie was old and hard, and it did not crumble. I was surprised to see my friend, who was in a hurry to leave. On the way out, he gave me his number and told me he was staying in a nearby motel. Though he was living only some twenty-five miles away, we did not have much opportunity to meet each other, and I was surprised to see him in my town. I thought he might know the techy stuff, and this would be a good opportunity to connect with him. When I called him, he was about to leave for somewhere but had a few minutes for me. When I asked whether he knew the meaning of TTTO message, he quickly responded that it meant TimeTo Throw Out.

I was not sure what should be thrown out: my computer, the outfit, or the dryer. I asked my friend what to throw out. He told me that it depended on where I got the message from and added his wife got that from her psychologist, and that is why she had thrown him out, and he is in a motel. As he was talking, the garage door opened, indicating my wife's arrival, and I got a panic attack and passed out in my chair, murmuring TTTO . Coming in, she saw the outfit in my hand and me muttering TTTO. She thanked me for picking up the outfit for the garbage. Hearing that, I perked up. She went on to say that she had scanned the QR Code of the outfit and it revealed that it had passed the fashion expiry date. She further added if this outfit had not cleared the house that day, the radio frequency identification would have flagged her in the website. Without wasting a moment, she told me she was going to a meeting of an E-Book club and told me on her way out 'TTYL'.

I fainted again in disbelief, this time muttering TTTO TTYL. All along, my friend was listening, and he shouted from the other end "You have now become the originator of TTBB TTYN club". All perplexed, I asked him to explain.

Yes, he said, "You started Time To Throw Out Talk To You Later (TTTO TTYL) and Time To Bring Back Talk To Me Now (TTBBTTMN) Club." He declared he had already been a member and rushed to go to talk to his wife. Suddenly I found myself elevated to the founder of an elite club. Before leaving, he suggested that it would be cool as a founder if I had the QR code of the club tattooed on me. The thought of the needles poking frightened me, and I shouted out loud, "No," and that is when my wife woke me up and asked whether I had a bad dream. Realizing I was in bed all this time, I told her TTYL and rushed to the washroom. She pulled me and told me, "Talk to me now." I was in shock and shouted, "OMG, you knew it!" And I fainted!

Chapter 12: Rocket Science learnt in a different MIT

After the celebrations of the successful landing of Chandrayaan on the moon's surface, a lot of attention was paid in India, to the people behind the project. There were back-and-forth arguments in newspapers, blogs, and WhatsApp groups as to which technology institutes, the National Institutes (NITs) or the Indian Institutes (IIT) of Technology contributed more towards the project.

For a commerce graduate with no formal science or engineering background, my introduction to rocket science happened at MIT (Mannarkoil Institute of Technology, located in my village of birth Mannarkoil). I know I am following the footsteps of the famous story teller of Malgudi Days fame R.K.Narayanan. He named the cricket club of his imaginary town Malgudi as MCC to sound like The MCC of London. I hope R.K Narayan's Talkative Man will not take me to court for using M for a place other than Malgudi. I guess I can take a chance.

Let me come to the rocket science. In the village, we used to roam around the backyards and pick up immature coconut fruits. These are not the tender coconuts that the street vendors sell after chopping the top, poking a hole and sticking in a bent plastic straw so that you can drink the coconut water. These fall off the tree much before the inner shell and the extra-cellular fluid are developed. We call it kurumbai (குரும்பை) in Tamil.

A blend of green, yellow and orange in colour, and with smooth outer skin, these immature fruits fall due to a variety of reasons that include heavy wind, monkeys playing on the tree, collateral damage during harvest of matured fruit bunches, and of course the natural course of aborted delivery. Whatever the reason, they were fun to play with. We would remove the petal-like cover to expose the creamy white soft surface. By the side of the tree, there would be plenty of scattered leaflets. We would carefully examine and pick the ones that had a strong but pliable midrib. We would tear off the leaf parts, take the midrib, and stick the broader/ stronger end all the way down into the middle of the fruit.

Voila- we had a rocket in our hand, ready to launch.

We used to hold the fruit by the loose end of the mid-rib, give it a few swings and throw it with all the strength we had. With a hissing sound, our rocket would take off and come down in a few seconds; more often than not, they were reusable for a few more launches. If our rocket could go as far as the top of the coconut tree, we would be thrilled. Those of us who could not shoot it up would swing the rocket two or three times around our head and throw horizontally like a hammer throw.

All our fun ended when we sighted the landlord uncle (no relation but a generic uncle) walking back from his farm, followed by his servant five feet behind. That was because of what had happened a few days earlier.

Uncle used to have a routine of evening inspection of his farm. Dressed in his white dhoti, white shirt and a long, thin white towel around the neck, he would walk majestically carrying an umbrella. The umbrella had a nice wooden handle and a sharp conic metallic tip at the end. His pace could be measured by the umbrella tip marks as he used the umbrella almost like a walking stick. His servant was a muscular man in a dhoti and a thick black belt around the dhoti. The belt had a pouch with a knife. He was bare-chested, with his towel tied around his hips. He would follow the landlord with a bagful of harvested fruits such as mangoes, lemons, coconuts, etc. A few days earlier, when the uncle was returning from his farm visit, one of our rockets almost landed on his head. He had a round, shiny bald head, and if we define the front side as east, our rocket would have landed on the south pole near his right earlobe. Given his tender scalp, it would have made a permanent mark on landing, and we could have claimed to be pioneers in launching a rocket on the south pole of the moon.

But he has seen many moons, and by reflex he used his umbrella like a cricket bat and deflected the rocket and smoothly grounded it. We were petrified, and about to take off, when he disarmed us with his smile and bragged how he had used the umbrella like the dead and defensive bat of the cricketer Manjurekar. As we were mentally thanking Manjurekar and about to take a sigh of relief, he issued a stern warning that we should have our rocket game on a faraway ground and not on a street corner with a lot of traffic. Besides that, he was clear that it was time for us to go home and get back to studies as it was dark already.

This landlord was a unique character. He had no kids, but he was kid-friendly. He was the only one of his age group in the street who had gone to college, and he used to brag about his cricket skills. Due to personal circumstances, he had returned to the village before completing his B.A. He was generous to share his experience with youngsters and give good advice. Of course, one had also to be patient enough to listen to his heroics. He would narrate how brave he had been in pinning a cobra to the ground with the tip of his umbrella until his servant could come with a stick and hit the snake. In fact, he told us the snake was buried in his garden with a small stone marking the place, and he offered milk to the stone every Friday as the cobra was a form of Lord Vishnu. He used to say that the snake spat so much venom on the umbrella tip that some rats died when he touched them with his umbrella! Maybe, much before the Russians, he had learnt the technology of killing a rat with a poisoned umbrella!

I am digressing. This is where I remember my Grade seven teacher, Mr. Vaidyanatha Iyer. He taught us a trick: "If you prepare well for an essay on coconut tree but the exam question is on a cow, do not get panicky," he used to say. "Start the essay by saying cows are generally tied to a coconut tree and write everything about the coconut tree that you have prepared well."

It is in his class that I gathered additional insight on aerodynamics. Vaidynatha Iyer was short, well-built and had a tuft. During lunchtime, it was a sight for us to see him letting his hair down and tying it back. His tuft was neither bun-shaped nor cone-shaped but something in between, like a croissant. Whenever he turned towards the chalkboard, his tuft was a good target for the backbenchers to direct paper airplanes.

A number of factors, like the thickness of the paper, the sharpness of the point, the air that one blows in the middle hollow, and the thrower's arm strength, play a role in a successful launch. Whenever the teacher turned towards the chalkboard, a sortie of planes would go towards his tuft. The front benchers who would not participate in the launch would provide sound advice that the paper torn from a math notebook was better for the job. Math notebooks were special. They typically opened on a flip style rather than a turn style. The page had a small margin, a middle and another partition roughly at two-thirds of the page, reserving space for figures and rough work. The paper for the math notebook used to be thicker and would fold and hold well for a paper plane.

And finally, as, one of my friends Anand reminded me, as a part of continuing education, on every Deepavali, we practiced and upgraded our skill in the art and science of using a bottle to control the launch direction of a rocket.

Given all this, I can boldly say that the contributor to our successful launch of Chandrayaan is our VITs- Village Institute of Technologies, and MIT happened to be one such VIT.

PS

Several years ago, a famous Tamil movie director, A.P. Nagarajan- who is known for mythological movies- directed the movie Saraswathi Sabatham. This depicted the clash between three goddesses--Saraswathi, Lakshmi and Parvathi/Sakthi-- to determine which one--knowledge, wealth, or might –is the most important super-power.

It is rumoured that along similar lines, a movie is under production--IIT, NIT or MIT. Though it appears venture capitalists are betting on IITs, crowdfunding is backing a hitherto unknown VIT.

Chapter 13: Mannarkoil Syndrome

When I was growing up, I watched my brother suffer from frequent headaches. Whenever he visited us from the village, he would invariably arrive with a headache. The network of veins on his forehead would be prominent, and one could see the image of the number four. That must have been a sign, perhaps. Before hitting the couch, he would immediately do four things to handle his headache: take a tablet, have a cup of coffee, apply Amrutanjan, the pain balm, and tie a towel tightly around his head and lie down for a while. The tablet that he would reach for was Anacin, which depicted four fingers held up, on the sachet. It might appear that his headache and a clue for its remedy were visible on the forehead. I never understood why they used the expression 'written on the forehead' for one's fate. Was it because what was on the forehead was visible to everyone around but not the person concerned? Anyway, let me get back to the headache.

I started getting mild headaches on and off when I was in Grade ten. Some in the uncles and aunties network had talked to my family about how eyeglasses for their son took care of his headache. Keeping that in mind, the next time when I complained of a headache, an appointment with an eye doctor was promptly arranged. On the day of the appointment, by 9 o'clock in the morning, I arrived at the clinic of Dr. Krishnamoorthy, the eye doctor. He showed me a chair to sit on and put a few drops to dilate my eyes. He asked me to keep my eyes closed until his return and went away to the next room. He was a classical music fan and an amateur singer. He started a raga 'aalabana' (improv) in the next room. I was shaken up by the voice but remembered to keep my eyes closed. An assistant came to me and handed over a napkin to wipe out the drops that had escaped. I asked the assistant how long it would take before I could open my eyes. She told me that once the raga aalaabana was over, the doctor would come.

Whatever little Carnatic music I knew, I could make out that he was elaborating the raga Nilambari, a raga for sleep. My wicked mind thought that he was using his singing in the place of anesthesia for someone getting cataract surgery in the next room. Listening to radio concerts, I knew the aalabanas normally ran through thirty to forty minutes. I was ready for a nice nap. I was also thanking my stars that the doctor was not a Hindustani music lover who emulated Pandid Bhimsen Joshi. In that case, I would be sitting on the chair for hours.

More than three decades later, I was narrating the story of my singing ophthalmologist in a social gathering in Fredericton. A good number of my friends present thought that I was making it up. One of the guests, Dr. Shankaran, a urologist who was from a neighbouring town immediately asked me whether I was from Tirunelveli. I was surprised as to how he knew. He told me that he was from Tirunelveli and he revealed the secret that the singing ophthalmologist was his cousin! I did not have the courage to ask him whether he himself used aalabana to break the kidney stones of his patients! I could not crack a joke at his expense when he had vouched for the veracity of my story.

The eyeglasses prescribed were of minimal power. Whether it had a real effect or a placebo effect, it seemed to have worked in relieving my headache. I was also happy to have a pair of glasses as it gave a scholarly (or nerdy?) image. A major difficulty I faced was in science classes whenever I had to look through a microscope. I could not place my eyes properly and adjust the focus appropriately; hence, the telescopes kept in tourist attractions near the Kodak photo points never attracted me either. I guess I have saved a few dollars!

The effect of eyeglasses in controlling my headache started waning. After about ten years, when I was working in Ahmedabad, my headaches started coming back. If I did not have lunch in time, or when I had a particular preparation of potato that came with 'poori,' or if I was constipated the previous day, I would get headaches. The headaches were more severe than those I had during school days, and I could feel the bulging of my veins. I remembered my brother's four formulas. I had some coffee, took a tablet, applied Amrutanjan and tied a cloth around my head. There were two major differences. The tablet I went for was a micro-fined Aspro that came in a red sachet. And I used a 'banian' as a headband and not a towel.

We boys in our family used banians that had sleeves. One of the major reasons for wearing a banian was to protect our shirts from sweat, and hence, an RNS or round-neck sleeved banian was our go-to undershirt. As we used to sweat a lot in the collar and armpits area, those parts of the banians would have received heavy doses of soap and beatings over time. As they develop holes around those areas, the banians would be relegated to other uses, such as cleaning a fountain pen or bicycle.

I would tie the banian around my head and tie a knot tightly to the point of throbbing. The sleeves part of the banian would be hanging in front of my eyes like a shade. I would lie down and try to press the tight knot hard on my pillow, giving pseudo acupressure as an additional treatment. The modified four-point programme was working all right.

When I moved to Fredericton, the headaches started coming more frequently, and I could not pinpoint them to any particular cause. I went to my family physician. Listening to my history, she felt that what I had was a migraine headache. She gave a prescription for a pill to be taken when the headache was severe. On my next migraine attack, I took the pill, and the relief was very quick. However, the headache reappeared after a day and the length of the attacks lingered over a couple of days, though with reduced intensity.

That gave me some concern, and on investigation, I found out that one of the ingredients of the pill was codeine, and that had a side effect of constipation. Given that constipation is one of my triggers for the headache, I could connect the dots. The pill would induce constipation, and that might have caused the secondary attack. I realized the danger of getting into a vicious circle of popping pills to mitigate headaches, resulting in headaches.

In the meantime, I started hearing noises in my ear. Concerned about tinnitus, I consulted an ENT specialist. After checking thoroughly, he indicated that I did not have tinnitus, but what I had in the ear was migraine. He explained that migraine was not confined to the head and was related to any vascular inflammation. Though relieved that my ears were all right, I came out very confused.

Finally, I thought I would check with my close friend's daughter, who is a neurologist, as to what the cause of my headaches was and what I should do. At the outset, she tried to dismiss me by saying she did not deal much with headaches. Rather, she was a movement disorder person. Nevertheless, as general advice, she asked me to take

Tylenol very early in the attack rather than waiting for the headache to become unbearable. I was not willing to give up easily. I countered her, saying my headache moved from one side to the other side of the forehead and should be covered under movement disorder.

She replied,"Uncle, I deal with muscular disorders and what you have is vascular." Given my hissing in the ears, I thought she said something to the effect of muscular. Hence, I pestered her, saying, "My temporal muscles move when I get headache, and if you are dealing with muscular movements, you should know."

Realizing that I would not take no for an answer, she asked me to sit down and provide her with the history. I started with the story of my singing ophthalmologist, my headache due to hunger and eating spice, my discovery of the constipation-codeine loop and the headache in my ears. After listening carefully, she declared that my headache was idiopathic.

Due to my distorted hearing, I got annoyed and asked, "Are you saying I am on an idiot's path in searching for an answer?"

She laughed and laughed and said, "I did not say idiot's path; I said idiopathic, and that is physicians' way of saying they do not know. Patients will not be happy if a doctor says he does not know. The bottom line to your question is I do not know."

I could not handle her response and shot back. "I now know my good friend and your dad is an idiot. Instead of spending his money on your study of four years of neuroscience, another four years of medicine and five years of neurology for you to respond 'I do not know the answer' he should have put his money elsewhere. That would have given him enough income to give you a very good life and sponsor me to consult a super-specialist."

Looking at my agitated state, she told me she would send me to a team-based clinic specializing in headaches. Apart from clinical history, they might even do a functional MRI to observe how I reacted to certain verbal and visual stimuli, etc.

In a couple of days, I visited the specialized clinic. "Hello, Mr. Gopalan," greeted the doctor. Right away I told him Gopalan was not my first name and joked he would be calling me Mannarkoil if I had added the village initials as was the custom in South India. As I was rattling out my naming stories, the assistants prepared me to get inside the MRI machine with headphones to provide audio clues. In parallel, another member of the team was going over the history as forwarded by my friend's daughter, and another was going through my medications. The team seemed to be busy. Inside the MRI machine, I was in a trance, thanks to the closed space and the noise. However, it appeared I was listening and responding.

After the tests were over, I was waiting in the doctor's office. He came back with a few pages of the report and told me what I had was Mannarkoil Syndrome. It was a type of thought-induced viral attack. There was a dormant Malgudi virus in my system that got activated by nostalgia and long winding narrative sentences, and that I really got hyper-charged with the word Mannarkoil. Like other viruses, this mutation also was in search of new hosts. Just like sneezing gets the cold virus out, writing and talking about the thoughts would give relief, and no other medication was needed.

The epidemiologist in the team had produced a quick report. The reproduction rate of the virus R_o (R naught) was very low. Contact tracing indicated no risk of high level of spread of the infection. Ninety percent of the recipients of the bug were not likely to re-transmit, and a very small percentage might get into a back-and-forth contact loop. The strength of the virus would diminish with each iteration, and hence, the risk of an epidemic was very small. However their ChatGPT report had indicated that the virus could get high strength if processed through an aromatic incense called *Sambrani*!

The target population at risk was people above fifty and those who had been infected by Malgudi virus earlier were at high risk. The newer generation of people were immune to the virus attack. That was because they had taken an X vaccine, which prevented them from recognizing long words and phrases exceeding one hundred and forty characters.

Happy to know the name of my disease, I came back to tell my friend's daughter. I expressed my surprise as to how quickly the specialist team diagnosed my ailment. I wondered that she was not aware of Mannarkoil syndrome. Once again, she laughed out loud. I asked her what the matter was. She asked me whether I remembered the joke I used to tell her about an assistant professor, an associate professor and a professor. It went something like this: "An assistant professor is one who will run a whole class with one point, an associate will run a term, and a full professor the whole career with one point," I said. "It is similar," she said. "We physicians have a hierarchy. A generalist, instead of saying I do not know, will send a patient to a specialist. Specialists will say idiopathic for things they do not know. If the patient persists, we send him to a super-specialist with a note that the patient will not take no for an answer. They will simply call it a syndrome named after the persistent patient." Hearing this, I was aghast. "In due course, a syndrome will become a disorder and then a disease, but we will not know the cause," she continued.. "Do not think too much. Otherwise, you will get a headache," was her advice. "And by the way, uncle," said she, "there is a note saying they tried to name it after Gopalan, but Gopalan Syndrome was already taken, and they do not like any name where S and R come next to each other as there is no word in English that has them together. Hence, they ruled out Srini Syndrome and went for Mannarkoil Syndrome. Besides, they had observed a high level of activity in your brain when that word was pronounced."

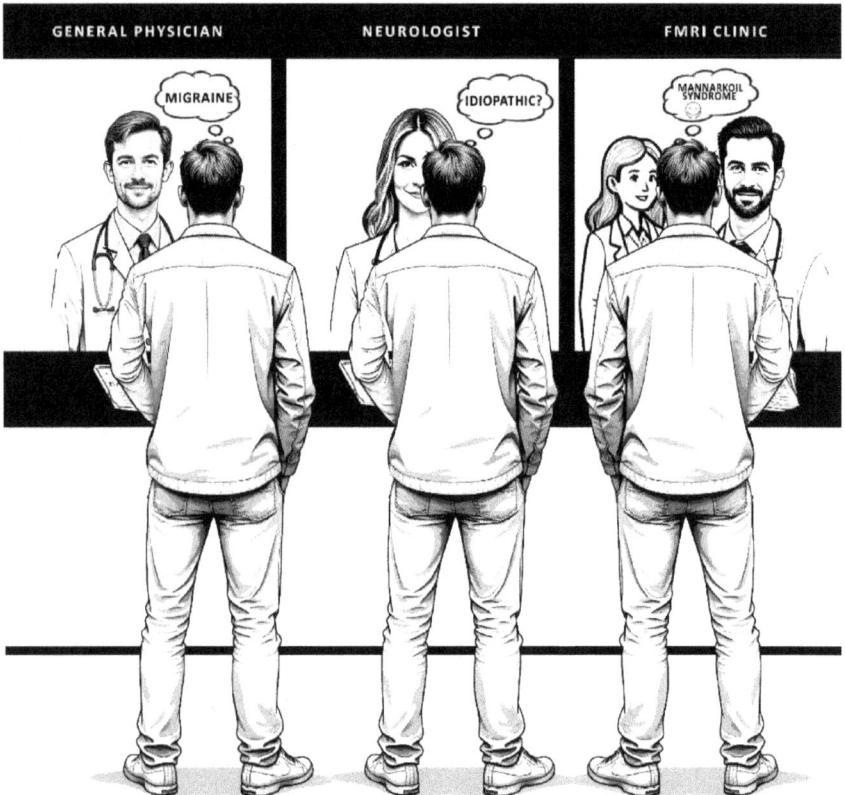

All these conversations were going above my head, and I sat with my hand on my forehead. I felt the number four on my forehead. Thinking forearmed is forewarned, I immediately rushed for my four-point solution for Mannarkoil Syndrome-induced headache! As the doctor ordered, I started to write and speak to get the virus out.

MANNARKOIL SYNDROME

About the Author

Gopalan Srinivasan was born in Mannarkoil village in Tirunelveli district of Tamil Nadu, India. After having his early education in Tirunelveli, he did his doctoral programme at the Indian Institute of Management Ahmedabad (IIMA). He worked at IIMA for a few years before moving to Canada. He joined the University of New Brunswick (UNB) Fredericton Business Faculty, where he taught over three decades. Currently he is leading a retired life in Missisauga Ontario with his wife and life partner Kalyani.

www.ingramcontent.com/pod-product-compliance
Lightning Source LLC
Chambersburg PA
CBHW060757050426
42449CB00008B/1430